Making Sense in Psychology and the Life Sciences

Margot Northey & Brian Timney

Making Sense in Psychology and the Life Sciences

a student's guide to

research, writing, and style

Toronto   OXFORD UNIVERSITY PRESS   1995

Oxford University Press, 70 Wynford Drive, Don Mills, Ontario M3C 1J9

Oxford   New York
Athens   Auckland   Bangkok   Bombay   Calcutta   Cape Town
Dar es Salaam   Delhi   Florence   Hong Kong   Instanbul   Karachi
Kuala Lumpur   Madras   Madrid   Melbourne   Mexico City
Nairobi   Paris   Singapore   Taipei   Tokyo   Toronto

and associated companies in
Berlin   Ibadan

Oxford is a trademark of Oxford University Press

Canadian Cataloguing in Publication Data

Northey, Margot, 1940–
   Making sense in psychology and the life sciences

2nd ed.
Includes index.
ISBN 0-19-541094-7

1. Psychology – Authorship.   2. Life sciences – Authorship.
3. Report writing.   I. Timney, Brian.   II. Title.

BF76.7.N67   1995   808'.06615   C95-930980-2

1 2 3 4 5 – 99 98 97 96 95

Printed in Canada

Contents

Acknowledgements

In preparing this second edition of *Making Sense in Psychology and the Life Sciences*, we have incorporated suggestions from users in every part of the country. The enthusiasm of many students and their instructors provided the impetus to keep improving. We are grateful for their constructive criticism. We also thank Walter Zimmerman of the D.B. Weldon Library at the University of Western Ontario who provided helpful comments on the chapter on obtaining information. Finally we thank Sally Livingston for all her thoughtful editorial assistance.

Symbols for common errors

NOTE: If any of the following markings appear on one of your essays or reports, consult Chapter 10, 11, or 12, or the Glossary, for help.

agr agreement of subject and verb

amb ambiguity

awk awkwardness

cap capitalization

cs comma splice

dang dangling modifier (*or* dm)

D diction

gr grammar (*or* usage)

mod misplaced modifier

new paragraph

// parallelism

ref punctuation

P pronoun reference

quot quotation marks

rep repetition

RO run-on sentence

frag sentence fragment

SS sentence structure

sp spelling

sp inf split infinitive

sub subordination

T tense

trans transition

∽ transpose (change order of letters or words)

wdy wordy

ww wrong word

A note to the student

Contrary to many students' belief, good writing does not come naturally; even for the best writers it's mostly hard work, following the old formula of ten per cent inspiration and ninety per cent perspiration. Writing in university or college is not fundamentally different from writing elsewhere. Yet each piece of writing has its own special purposes, and these are what determine its shape and tone. *Making Sense in Psychology and the Life Sciences* will examine both the general precepts for effective writing and the particular requirements of writing papers in psychology (especially the research paper and the lab report); it will also point out some of the most common errors in student composition and suggest how to avoid or correct them.

Throughout this edition we have placed a much greater emphasis on the style guidelines provided in the fourth edition of the *Publication Manual of the American Psychological Association*, the gold standard for most writers in psychology. We have included a new chapter on APA style and one dealing with ethical issues in research and writing.

Although we have followed the *APA Manual* with respect to format, the advice we offer is in the form of guidelines rather than strict rules, because few rules are inviolable. We hope that this book will help you escape the common pitfalls of student writing and develop confidence through an understanding of basic principles and a mastery of sound techniques. The intent of the original *Making Sense* remains: to give you a clear, concise, and readable guide that will help you do well on all your courses.

1

Writing for a

scientific audience

One of your most frustrating experiences as a student likely occurs when you get back an essay or lab report only to find that the grade is much lower than you expected. Sometimes, when you ask why, your instructor will tell you: "It didn't hang together very well," or "You seemed to know the material, but you didn't get your points across as well as some other students." Often an instructor will not go into any detail about how you might have improved your paper, so you are thrown back onto your own devices. This can be especially irritating for the science student, who may have less opportunity to write papers than an arts or social-science student. It may seem unfair that someone who knows less about the material than you do gets a better mark because the instructor seems to give unnecessarily strong emphasis to "writing style."

Although many instructors do place a premium on style, it is important to realize that good writing is not just correct grammar and spelling. These things do make a difference, but it is also important that you express your ideas in a clear and logical way. Your instructors are not mind readers. You cannot leave out some connecting links in an argument and still expect to get credit. Nor should you take it for granted that just because your instructors know the topic, they will understand what you're talking about. They may, but their job is to evaluate what you have written, not what they think you want to say.

The primary purpose of this book is to provide some guidelines that will help you to develop your scientific writing skills. Rather than simply tell you the best way to express yourself, we have tried to set this information into the context of active science, starting with the assumption that people write better if they know what their readers are looking for.

Science places a high value on your capacity to organize information and present it concisely. The best science writers have the ability to describe a complicated theory or procedure in a way that not only makes it easy to understand, but also conveys their own interest in, and excitement about, their material. This is not a skill that some people just happen to be born with. Although not everyone can write like Stephen Jay Gould or the late Lewis Thomas, almost anyone can learn to write in a way that will convince the reader that the author is scientifically literate and has a good grasp of the subject.

Perhaps the most important aspect of scientific writing is that it is research-driven. Whenever you write an essay, a review paper, or a lab report, you will be describing research, whether it is your own or someone else's. Over the years, science has developed a set of implicit and explicit rules for such writing. Minor details may vary from one discipline to another, but it should be possible for a physicist or a psychologist to read a biology paper and judge whether the science is reasonable, even if they don't understand all the technical details.

Scientific thinking and scientific writing

No matter whether you are writing an essay in English, a review paper in microbiology, or a lab report in psychology, you are not likely to produce clear writing unless you have first done some clear thinking. This means first working out what you want to say, and then organizing your thoughts in a coherent way before you commit them to paper. For the most part, the ability to write clearly is independent of subject material or form. But there are occasional exceptions. Sometimes we encounter a student who can produce an excellent essay, but whose lab reports are a disaster. Different rules apply to different kinds of writing, and it is essential to take these into account.

In scientific writing it is especially important to express yourself clearly, because much of the time you will be trying to convey complex factual information. To convince your reader that you know what you're talking about, you have to ensure that he or she can understand what you've written. To do this, you must think about not only what you want to say, but how you are going to say it.

In some ways the distinction between the kinds of writing done by a biologist, or a psychologist, or a historian is artificial. Each is concerned with telling a story based on empirical evidence that has been gathered, sorted, and evaluated in a logical, systematic way. The only differences lie in the kind of evidence that is looked at and the specific rules used to evaluate it. In fact, it is possible to be scientific in your approach to almost any academic discipline; all you have to do is ensure that your evidence is complete and your analysis of it systematic and logical.

On the other hand, it is also possible to approach even "scientific" subject matter in a way that is anything but scientific. Perhaps the best way to see the difference between scientific and non-scientific writing is to compare the descriptions of a particular finding in a scholarly journal and a tabloid newspaper. In a tabloid, scientific discoveries are typically presented as established facts, with no attempt to evaluate how the data were gathered or whether the conclusions are justified. The story may be written in correct English, but no science instructor would be satisfied with it.

For example, a newspaper story on a new drug treatment for cancer might even suggest that this is the cure everyone has been searching for. If you were to look up the original report in a medical journal, however, you might find that the treatment worked only for certain types of cancer, that the number of patients who improved was quite small, and that the authors put all kinds of qualifiers on their conclusions. After reading the newspaper article you might think that a cure for cancer had been found. After reading the journal article you would be more likely to conclude that this was just another small step in the scientific investigation of cancer. What this example shows is that to be scientific, a report must not only present the author's own evaluation of the evidence; it must also provide enough information for readers to draw their own conclusions.

Initial strategies

Before you even consider what you will write, you should ask yourself two basic questions:

• What is the purpose of this piece of writing?
• Who is my target audience?

Think about the purpose

Writing a review of a body of literature requires a different approach from a paper in which you are considering the merits of two opposing theories. Sometimes you will be asked to *discuss* a particular topic, sometimes to *compare* different viewpoints. At other times you may be writing a lab report or a thesis. Each of these will require a different approach. Even if you select your own topic, you must decide how you will write your paper.

Depending on the assignment, your purpose will be one (or more) of the following:

- to describe and interpret an experiment you have done;
- to show that you can do independent library research;
- to show that you understand certain terms or theories;
- to show that you can think clearly and critically.

Think about the reader

Even if the only person who will read your paper is your instructor, don't think of that one individual as your target audience. If you do, you're likely to leave out important details of an explanation because you assume your instructor will know what you're talking about. Instead, try to think of your reader as someone who is knowledgeable in the discipline but doesn't know everything about your specific topic. Again, the person who reads your paper can read only what is on the page, not what is in your head. Don't take detailed knowledge about your topic for granted.

Thinking about the reader also means taking into account the intellectual context in which he or she operates. If you were to write a paper on human sexuality for a biology course, it would be quite different from one on the same topic submitted for a psychology course. You have to make specific decisions about the background information you will supply, the terms you will need to explain, and the amount of detail that is appropriate for a given situation. When you are writing a lab report you need to give much more procedural detail than you would if you were writing a review of the same topic. If you don't know who will be reading your paper—your professor, your tutorial leader, or a marker—just imagine someone intelligent, well-informed and interested, skeptical enough to question your ideas, but flexible enough to accept them if your evidence is convincing.

Think about the length

Before you start writing, you will also need to think about the length of the assignment in relation to the time you have available to spend on it. If both the topic and the length are prescribed, it should be fairly easy for you to assess the level of detail required and the amount of research you need to do. If only the length is prescribed, that restriction will help you decide how broad or how narrow a topic you should choose.

Think about the tone

In everyday writing to friends you probably take a casual tone, but academic writing is usually more formal. The exact degree of formality will depend upon the kind of assignment and instructions you have been given. In some cases—for example, if your psychology professor asks you to keep a journal describing certain personal experiences—you may well be able to use an informal style. In lab reports and review papers, however, where you need to express yourself unambiguously, a more formal tone is required. On the other hand, you should also avoid the other extreme of excessive formality.

What kind of style is inappropriate for most scientific writing? Here are some pointers:

Use of slang. There are very few occasions when the use of a slang word or phrase is appropriate in a science paper. If you described a rat moving quickly down the one arm of a maze as "going like a bat out of hell," you might convey the wrong impression to a reader. Another reason for not using slang expressions is that they are often regional and short-lived: they may mean different things to different groups at different times. (Just think of how widely the meaning of the terms *hot* and *cool* can vary, depending upon the circumstances).

Frequent use of contractions. Generally speaking, contractions such as "can't" and "isn't" are not suitable for scientific writing, although they may be fine for letters or other informal kinds of writing —for example, this handbook.

Excessive use of first-person pronouns. If you are writing a lab report about an experiment that you have done, there is no need to keep reminding the reader of this fact. However, you could use first-person pronouns occasionally if the choice is between using *I* or *we* and creating a tangle of passive constructions. (A hint: when you do use *I*, it will be less noticeable if you place it in the middle of the sentence rather than at the beginning.)

Excessive use of long words and jargon. Perhaps the worst sin of scientific writing—and it is by no means confined to fledglings in the field—is the use of jargon that is unintelligible to the uninitiated.

"Never use a short word if a longer, more esoteric one will do" seems to be a general rule for many scientific writers. If your writing seems stiff or pompous, you may be relying too much on jargon, high-flown phrases, long words, or passive constructions. Although sometimes you must use specialized terms to avoid long and complex explanations, the rest of your paper can be written in simple English. At first glance it may not appear so impressive, but it will certainly be a lot easier to understand.

The following passage appeared in a recent PhD thesis that one of us examined:

> By ameliorating schizophrenic proclivity toward inefficiently deploying their attentional capacity, it is not beyond the realm of possibility that this population could become closer to healthy individuals in terms of cognitive and behavioral functioning.

Roughly translated, what this means is "If people with schizophrenia could pay more attention, they might be better off." Cutting away the dead wood produces a clear statement that the reader can evaluate on its own merits.

2

Library research

One of the most important rules in writing a scientific paper is that everything you say must be supported by documentary evidence. This rule applies whether you're writing a lab report for a classroom project or a review paper for publication in a professional journal. If you're going to make a career as a scientist, you will quickly find out that you must be able to back up your arguments with facts. When you are just starting out in university, your assignments will probably not require extensive library research. However, once you've learned how to track down information efficiently, you'll find that this skill is a powerful asset in many different situations.

Where to start

Let's assume that you have already selected—or been assigned—a topic to write about. (More details about planning a paper are given in Chapter 4.)

Your first task is to find out the names of the major authors in your field. Once you have this information, you can begin to look more systematically for relevant papers. If you have absolutely no knowledge about your topic, perhaps the best way to start is to take the shotgun approach—look everywhere, but do it superficially. There are quite a few ways to get at least a general idea of what is going on in a particular area.

Ask other people

It's surprising, but not many students take advantage of their primary resource-person: their course instructor. Although you should not expect to be provided with all the information you will need, your instructor should be able to give you some names and references to get you started. Similarly, if you have a graduate teaching assistant, or even friends who know more than you do about a particular topic, don't be afraid to ask.

Browse around the library

One strategy for getting an overview is to browse through some of the primary and secondary sources in a field. For example, let's say that you wanted to write an essay on congenital insensitivity to pain. You know that the literature on pain is vast, and you also know that there is relatively little information on congenital insensitivity. You might try the following approach:

1. Look at the subject heading index in your library's catalog system. You might start with "pain" as a general heading, or you could try to narrow your search by looking at terms such as "pain—insensitivity" or "hypoalgesia" or "analgesia." A quick glance through the catalog will show you that most of the books on pain have similar call numbers.

2. Once you find the appropriate stack, just browse through some of the textbooks that are there. You don't have to look for specific titles: just go through the indexes of different books for any reference to pain insensitivity. Even if you don't find a full book on your specific subject, you should find a few relevant references; you'll also begin to see how different authors have discussed the topic.

3. Another place to start is in the specialized journals dealing with your topic. Much of the research on pain is published in the journal *Pain*. If you go to the current periodicals section of your library and skim through the contents pages of all of the issues for the past year or so, you might find something useful. This technique doesn't always work, but when it does it can give you a lot of information. Not only will you have an up-to-date reference on a topic, but the reference list at the end of the paper will provide other recent references.

Systematic searching

The strategies outlined above will help you get some start-up information. If you are writing a review of a body of literature, however, you will need to obtain a much more extensive list of references. You can do this in two ways: manually, as described below, or by doing a computer-based search, which we will describe in the following section.

Manual searches

Secondary sources

If someone has written a review paper or chapter on your topic in the last few years, it may provide a listing of the earlier literature on that subject; then you can concentrate on tracking down more recent references. You can often find references to review papers by checking your textbooks, or simply asking your professor. If these approaches fail, you may still be able to get some leads in the library.

One of the best sources is the *Index of Scientific Reviews*. This is a serial publication listing review articles and chapters that have appeared in the recent scientific literature. Sources are filed under different subject headings and are extensively cross-referenced, so if you are not sure of the best way to describe what you are looking for, you can find alternative headings here.

Another useful source is the "Annual Review" series. These are books of reviews that are published each year and provide detailed summaries of current research. The series includes the *Annual Review of Psychology*, the *Annual Review of Neuroscience*, the *Annual Review of Physiology*, the *Annual Review of Genetics*, and the *Annual Review of Entomology*. These volumes are particularly helpful because they cover most of the subareas of a discipline, and new reviews are commissioned every few years.

In psychology there are a number of publications that will help you begin your search, whether for topics or for references. If you are looking for a topic to write on, you could consult a handbook, such as the *Handbook of social psychology* (Lindzey & Aronson, 1985), *Stevens' handbook of experimental psychology* (Atkinson, Herrnstein, Lindzey, & Luce, 1988), or the *Handbook of psychological assessment* (Goldstein & Hersen, 1990). Each of these gives a broad overview of the field and may provide you with ideas for topics to write about.

Abstract and index journals

When you are forced to look for all your references from scratch, one of the most thorough (although not the most efficient) approaches is to use the abstract or index journals. You will find a surprising number of such journals in the reference section of your library. Covering almost every major subdivision of the social and life sciences, they range from *Aquatic Sciences and Fisheries Abstracts* to *Weed Abstracts*. Among the most useful are *Biological Abstracts, Excerpta Medica, Index Medicus, Psychological Abstracts,* and *Social Sciences Index.*

Abstract journals contain numbered listings of abstracts of publications organized under a wide variety of headings and subheadings. If you know which heading your topic of interest might fall under, you simply look this up in the subject index to obtain the numbers of the abstracts that deal with the topic. Then you can look through each of the abstracts to see if it is relevant to your needs. You can do the same thing with index journals, such as *Index Medicus*, except that these list only basic information about the publication, without an abstract.

Although you can obtain a tremendous amount of information by searching the abstracts and indexes, it can be a time-consuming and frustrating procedure. In order to get a few references on your topic, you may have to look through an awful lot of irrelevant information. You can often spend a whole afternoon in the library and not have much to show for it. On the positive side, however, an abstract search will often turn up papers that you might not have found otherwise. Also, you may find that, after spending some time browsing through the abstracts, you begin to recognize some of the important names in the field and the kinds of experiments that people are doing.

Citation indexes

Another kind of index that allows you to find references, though in a somewhat different way, is the citation index. Two of these will be especially relevant to you: the *Science Citation Index* and the *Social Sciences Citation Index*. Unlike the subject-oriented abstracts and indexes described above, the citation indexes allow you to track down references through authors. They also let you search forward in time; that is, if you know of an important paper written by a certain author several years ago, you can find out who has referred to that paper since then.

Each of these indexes has several different sections, but the two most important for you will be the "Citation Index" and the "Source Index." To obtain information, you start by looking up the reference you know in the "Citation Index" section. This is your target article. Beneath it you will find an inventory of all the articles that have cited your target in that year; in addition to the author's name, each entry lists the journal in which the paper appeared, followed by the volume, page, and year. These citations, taken from the list of references at the end of each article, suggest that the authors may discuss something that is relevant to your topic. The more citations there are for a particular article, the more important it is likely to be.

Not every paper that cites your target article will be useful to you. But you have no way of knowing this at first, because the "Citation Index" gives only the location, not the title, of each article. To avoid wasting time in the library stacks, try looking at the "Source Index" section, which gives the title of every paper referred in the "Citation Index," listed by author. From there, you can look up the papers whose titles seem most promising. In turn, the reference lists of these papers may suggest additional sources. In this way you can build up a collection of core references that will allow you to make progressively wider searches—especially important if you are preparing the introduction to a thesis. For a short class essay, on the other hand, you can stop your search once you have identified the major papers in an area.

Computer-based searches

Almost every library now has its catalog in computer form. This means that you can do much more comprehensive searching than you could with just a card catalog. As a bonus, many libraries allow dial-in access to their catalogs from remote computers equipped with modems. If you have a modem, you don't have to leave the comfort of your own room to be able browse through the catalogs. You can even gain access to other library catalogs if you wish.

Online and CD-ROM databases

Most people are familiar with the computerized library catalogs, but there are also more powerful ways to gain access to information. Over the past few years, many of the abstract and index journals, such as *Science Citation Index*, *Index Medicus*, and *Psychological Abstracts*, have been stored as computer files that are accessible through your library's computer system. Hundreds of databases are now available, covering every conceivable topic. Your library will probably have access to several of these, depending on which services it subscribes to. Although online databases are used mostly by graduate students and faculty members, there is no reason not to use them for an undergraduate paper. For a short essay, obviously, you do not need to go to such lengths, but for a major research paper an online search is well worth considering.

Online databases are typically housed at some remote location, and your library will have dial-in access to them. Often this means that only library staff are allowed to do such searches. A more recent innovation is the CD-ROM database holding the entire contents of an abstract or index journal for several years. You may be able to borrow the CD to use at a computer in the library for a certain period of time. This is becoming an increasingly popular tool among undergraduates. Some of the most important abstract and index journals, such as *Psychological Abstracts* and *Index Medicus*, are available both online and on CD-ROM.

Why use an online database?

Although you can gather a tremendous amount of information from the abstract journals and citation indexes, it can be a slow, painful procedure. Your search will go much more quickly if you can automate it. There are three advantages to using such a system:

* speed of access;
* comprehensiveness of the search;
* access to sources that are not obvious, or not readily available.

With such vast amounts of information available, your biggest problem is restricting it to manageable levels. A careless search can produce hundreds of articles, most of which will be irrelevant to your needs. If the search is done properly, though, you may find most of the references you need in a surprisingly short period of time.

Rules for good computer searches

Because most online searches require connecting with a computer remote from the library, you may be better off allowing a librarian to do the searching on the basis of information that you provide: you discuss your needs with the searcher who sets up the most efficient search strategy. In fact, in some libraries this is the only way to get a search done. Typically, you will be charged for the computer time used, but unless it's a massive search the fees are not usually too high. In libraries that have CD-ROMs, on the other hand, you will probably be doing the search yourself. In that case you should know a little about the logic underlying database searches.

Although each database has its own particular rules, all require that you enter certain relevant keywords for which the computer can search. These may be contained in the title or the abstract of the paper, or they may be part of a list of *descriptors* assigned to the paper by an indexer. When you do a search you should use enough keywords to ensure that you do not miss large numbers of references, but not so many that you come up with a great deal of irrelevant material.

The most efficient way to do this is to use the rules of Boolean logic, which allows you to combine search terms using the logical operators *or*, *and*, and *not*. For example, suppose you had been assigned a biology paper on the feeding habits of blowflies. You might begin a general search using the terms "Blowfly or *Phormia regina*" and "Feeding or Hunger or Eating." This would give you a list of papers whose titles or descriptors contain some reference to blowflies in conjunction with feeding or eating. If this initial search produced too many references for your purposes, or if many of them were not closely related to what you were looking for, you could narrow the search by including more keywords such as "behavior," "taste," or "preference." By selecting the appropriate combination of search terms, a skilled searcher can usually come up with a moderate list of references, most of which will be of some use to you. (Remember that most of the databases come from the United States and use American spellings.) If you are having trouble establishing an appropriate search strategy, be sure to consult one of the reference librarians; that is what they are there for.

UnCover: A general purpose database

Although most psychology students are familiar with *PsycLIT*, the computerized version of *Psychological Abstracts*, and some of the other major databases, there is one more that can be very helpful. *UnCover* is a "table of contents" database that contains the information from the contents pages of thousands of journals and magazines from many different disciplines. It does not contain abstracts unless they are listed on the contents page, but it has many other advantages:

1. You can search for references in the same way that you do in *PsycLIT*, using keywords and names, but you can also use it to browse through the contents pages of specific journals.

2. If you're working in an area that crosses the boundaries between different disciplines—for example, in psychobiology or neuropsychology—the references you want may be contained in several different databases. Because *UnCover* is not specific to any discipline, it may provide most of what you want in a single search.

3. Unlike *PsycLIT*, whose use is usually restricted to the library, *UnCover* can be accessed through the Internet. This means that if you have a computer with a modem, or if you have access to your university computer system, you can get into *Uncover* independently.

4. *UnCover* is updated daily. This means that it is far more current than CD-ROMs, which may not be replaced for several months.

5. In addition to providing references, *UnCover* allows you to order papers directly. If a particular journal is not available in your library and you need a paper from it quickly, you can request the paper from *UnCover*. For a fee, they will fax it directly to you, in some cases within an hour or two of receiving your request. If your library subscribes to *UnCover*, you may be able to receive a discount price on any articles you order.

To gain access to *UnCover* from the Internet, all you need to do is to go into "telnet," then type *pac.carl.org*. From there you can follow the directions on the screen. For additional information consult your reference librarian.

References

Atkinson, R.C., Herrnstein, R.J., Lindzey, G., & Luce, R.D. (Eds). (1988). *Stevens' handbook of experimental psychology* (2nd ed., Vols. 1-2). New York: Wiley.

Goldstein, G., & Hersen, M. (Eds.). (1990). *Handbook of psychological assessment*. (2nd ed.). Elmsford, NY: Pergamon Press.

Lindzey, G., & Aronson, E. (Eds). (1985). *The handbook of social psychology* (3rd Ed., Vols. 1-2). New York: Random House.

3

Ethical issues in research

and writing

Until recently, there was a strong tendency for the average person to think of science as a "pure" endeavour and of scientists as disinterested individuals in pursuit of nothing but "truth." This is certainly the view of science promoted by those TV commercials in which a white-coated actor points to a set of "clinical studies" showing how effective a certain product is. In fact, however, science is not always driven by idealistic motives, and scientists are no different from other people. Some are interested above all in their research, and take great care in the way they go about it. Others, seeking primarily wealth and glory, may be willing to cheat to achieve those ends.

Outright scientific fraud is uncommon, but it is of sufficient concern that the U.S. National Institutes of Health have a special office devoted to investigating it. *Science* magazine, one of the most prestigious journals, now requires that investigators submitting a paper for publication have colleagues review it beforehand and make their data and materials available for verification.

For the most part, only the most glaring frauds reach the public through the media — usually when people are discovered to have falsified a significant part of their data. Stories of major scientific fraud emerge from time to time (Broad & Wade, 1982). However, most cases of questionable scientific behaviour are more prosaic: for example, a researcher may discard data from subjects who do not appear to be performing in accordance with expectations, or "adjust" a few data points to make the results look more impressive. Although such behaviour is obviously unacceptable, it almost certainly occurs at every level, from first-year undergraduate labs to major laboratories that are supported by millions of dollars in grant funds every year.

The purpose of discussing such unethical behaviour is not to disillusion you, but to start you thinking about what is right and wrong when you are working in the sciences. Later in this chapter we will return to the question of appropriate documentation of your work, but first we'll take a look at what constitutes ethical scientific research and reporting.

Ethical issues in the conduct of research

In the 1930s, a developmental psychologist interested in the role of experience in human development (Dennis, 1935; 1938) took over the care of a set of fraternal twins within a few weeks of their birth. Dennis (1935) explained that he did so "because the father failed to provide for them," and that "the mother understood that we offered temporary care of the twins in return for the privilege of studying them" (p. 18). Because he was interested in their motor development, the babies were kept lying on their backs in their cribs and were picked up only for feeding and changing. They were given no toys until they were 14 months old and were hand-fed so that they could not practice reaching. In addition, Dennis "kept a straight face in the babies' presence, neither smiling nor frowning, and never played with them, petted them, tickled them, etc." (p. 19).

That study was done long before anyone was aware of the effects of social deprivation on young children, and no doubt Dennis believed that what he was doing was in the children's best interests. But when we consider the research from today's perspective we are horrified. What this example shows is that, when we contemplate doing a study, we have to take into account its possible consequences.

When psychology students are first asked to carry out independent projects, they often propose to study the effects of drugs, alcohol, or exposure to sexually explicit materials on some aspect of behaviour. Although there is nothing intrinsically wrong with such studies, they do require that the researcher observe a strict code of conduct. Whenever any experiment is carried out using human subjects, two requirements must be fulfilled: there must be a good justification for doing the study, and the subjects who participate must be thoroughly informed about what they are getting into.

Justification

Although most studies conducted by professional researchers are driven by curiosity, for the most part they also have either a theoretical or a practical rationale. It is usually not enough to begin with the question "I wonder what would happen if. . . ." For one thing, most journals will not publish papers that do not offer a good rationale. In addition, when you try to write up a study of this kind, it is difficult to find anything useful to say in either your *Introduction* or your *Discussion*.

Today, all research projects involving humans or animals must be approved before they can be run. At the undergraduate level, the person giving approval may be either the course instructor or the chair of the department. In the case of research funded by a granting agencies, specific approval must be given by an ethics committee within the university. Depending on the kind of research, one or more different committees may be involved.

In general, the more invasive a study is, the stronger the justification must be. For example, a study to find out whether ingesting LSD improves a person's perception of colours would be less likely to be approved than a study of the effects of alcohol consumption on the detection of visual stimuli in a driving simulation test. Moreover, most institutions take the position that undergraduate projects must not have any potential to cause harm.

Informed consent and feedback

In addition to ensuring that your study is carried out carefully, you must always make certain that your subjects have a clear idea of what the study is about and understand that they have the right to refuse to participate, or to drop out mid-way through the experiment, if they wish. In almost all cases the researcher does this by preparing an *informed consent* form that describes the essential aspects of the study. The subjects read the form and sign it to indicate that they understand and accept the terms under which they will participate.

Typically, subjects will not be told the details of the experimental hypothesis at the beginning of the study, to reduce the risk of their influencing the outcome. In some studies it is even necessary to prevent subjects from knowing the main purpose of the experiment, because their knowledge would certainly affect the outcome. Such deception may be permitted if the investigator can justify it.

Whether the study involves deception or not, it is essential that at the end of it the subjects be given detailed feedback explaining exactly what the experiment was about. This is usually done by means of a feedback sheet that describes the study and provides references for follow-up. The experimenter should also be prepared to provide subjects with additional information if necessary.

Ethical issues in writing

When you carry out any piece of research, it is assumed that you will do it carefully, with appropriate regard to all ethical guidelines. Similar ethical standards are required for any written work you submit.

If you look through most university calendars you will find a section dealing with academic offences. These fall into three broad categories: *cheating* on examinations (which we will not discuss here), *fabrication*, and *plagiarism*. Penalties for academic dishonesty can be severe, ranging from a reprimand, through failure in the course, to expulsion from the university in the most serious cases. Despite these penalties, however, many students submit work that is not entirely their own.

Often it is easy to identify material that has been taken from elsewhere. First, the writing style of most students is usually different from that of the authors whose work they are copying. Second, the sources used by students are often so familiar to instructors that they will easily recognize where the material has been lifted from. In other cases, even if the writing style is not distinctive, the quality of the logic and argument may be well above what the instructor expects from a particular student. Following are some examples of what would be considered academic fraud on the part of a student.

Fabrication

Fabrication occurs when a student inserts false information into a paper. You will be fabricating information if you:

1. Invent data from an experiment you were supposed to conduct;

2. Pad a reference list or bibliography with sources you did not use in preparing the paper;

3. Include information that did not come from the cited source.

In each of these cases you are trying to gain credit for work you did not do. Submission of falsified data is treated as outright fraud. Even adding an extra reference here and there compromises the integrity of your work and is considered an academic offence.

Plagiarism

Plagiarism occurs when you present someone else's words, ideas, or data as your own. You are plagiarizing not only if you use direct quotations without attributing them to their source, but if you follow the structure and organization of someone else's work—that is, even if your words are completely different but you copy a theme, paragraph by paragraph, from someone else. You should also be aware that, even if you acknowledge your source, if you follow it too closely you may still be regarded as having copied from that person. Your work must be a product of your own thought processes, not just a minor modification of something you have read.

Examples of plagiarism range from paraphrasing of a sentence or two without appropriate acknowledgement of the source to submission of a paper that has been lifted wholesale from somewhere else. Discussions with students who have been accused of plagiarism reveal that many do not realize what is inappropriate. This results in what could be termed "inadvertent" plagiarism. A common cause of inadvertent plagiarism is the failure to record adequate information while taking notes from source materials. For example, you might have jotted down a series of direct quotes from a variety of sources while researching your topic, but failed to place them in quotation marks. Later, when writing up your essay, you may string together sentences and phrases from these research notes, forgetting that they are direct quotes. Even though you may not have intended to do anything dishonest, this is still plagiarism. At this stage of your academic career, ignorance is not a valid excuse: it is up to you to know the difference between original research and copying someone else's words and ideas.

Another situation in which students may be accused of plagiarism occurs when they have been asked to work on a project together but to do independent write-ups. In such cases students may copy directly from each other and submit reports that contain identical passages; or they may do the final write-up separately, but from an outline that they have prepared together. The result is two papers that are written in different words but whose organization and structure are identical. This too would be considered plagiarism. When you write a paper independently, all the creative aspects—not just the actual words— must be your own.

To give you a clear idea of what might be considered plagiarism, here are several examples, all based on the same original source, with some comments on why the student version is inappropriate.[1]

Source material:

Why would scientists want to study the brains of other animal species, if their ultimate goal is to learn about *human* thought and behavior? Scientists interested in how the nervous system controls behavior study other kinds of animals for three main reasons (Bullock, 1984). First, they do so to understand the evolutionary history, or phylogenetic roots, of the human brain. They trace what is old and what is new in the human brain—what evolution has brought about.

Second, they try to discover general rules or principles of brain function. Scientists who take this approach ask two different kinds of questions: (1) What in the nervous system correlates with known behavioral differences among animals? For example, if one species is aggressive and another is passive, what differences in their brains account for the difference? (2) What kinds of behavior correlate with known differences in the brains of animals? For example, if a certain brain structure is present in humans but not in other primates, or if a brain structure is larger in one species than another, how do these differences relate to behavior?

Third, scientists study the nervous systems of other animals to obtain information that is impossible to obtain from humans. Many studies that, for technical or ethical reasons, cannot be carried out in humans can be conducted in other animals. Animals provide scientists with "model systems" in which to address questions about how the human nervous system works because the nervous systems of humans and other animals are so much alike. . . .

(from Spear, Penrod, & Baker, 1988, pp. 29-30)

Direct quotation:

Why would researchers study the brains of lower animals, if their ultimate goal is to learn about human thought and behavior? Scientists interested in how the nervous system controls behavior study other kinds of animals for three main reasons (Bullock, 1984). First, they do so to understand the evolutionary history of the human brain, tracing what is old and what is new in the human brain. Second, they try to discover general rules or principles of brain function. Third, they study the nervous systems of other animals to obtain information that is impossible to obtain from humans. Many studies that cannot be carried out in other animals, for technical or ethical reasons, can be conducted in animals.

This is a clear example of plagiarism, in which the student has copied the source material almost verbatim, without any acknowledgement. The few minor changes in wording, and the omission of several phrases and sentences from the original, may have been intended to disguise the fact that this material was stolen.

Moreover, even if this passage were a paraphrase rather than a direct quote, the reference to Bullock (1984) would be inappropriate, because the student has evidently not drawn directly from this source, but has taken it from Spear et al. (1988). Rather than rely on secondary sources in this way, it is best to go to the original sources. The second-best solution would be to acknowledge the source as follows: (Bullock, 1984, as cited in Spear, Penrod, & Baker, 1988).

Paraphrase:

> In my view, there are three main reasons why scientists might study the brains of lower animals in order to learn about human brain function. First, by comparing the brains of animals at various levels of evolutionary development with those of humans, one can examine the evolutionary history of the human brain. Second, general rules or principles of brain function can be ascertained by examining ways in which behavioral differences between species are correlated with differences in their brain structures. Third, using lower animals for research allows scientists to conduct experiments that might be unethical if done on humans.

Even though the wording here is quite different from the source material, it still follows the train of thought of the original exactly. In failing to cite the source of these ideas, the student is making a false claim that they are his own. This dishonesty is compounded by beginning the paragraph with "In my view," which leads the reader to believe that the ideas are original.

Partial paraphrase:

> Why would scientists want to study the brains of other animal species, if they ultimately wish to learn about human thought and behavior? As Spear, Penrod, and Baker (1988) have pointed out, there are three main reasons for studying lower animals. First, scientists do so "to understand the evolutionary history, or phylogenetic roots, of the human brain." Second, this type of research allows for an examination of the general rules and principles of brain function, by examining ways in which behavioral differences between species are correlated with differences in their brain structures. Third, using lower animals for research allows scientists to conduct experiments that might be unethical if done on humans.

Here the student does cite the source of the material. However, she still does not adequately acknowledge the extent of her debt. Although part of one sentence is placed in quotation marks, several other sentences and phrases that are direct quotes from the original have not been placed in quotation marks. A paraphrase must be entirely the words of the writer; any borrowed words or phrases must be placed in quotation marks. In addition, the student has failed to point out that Spear, Penrod, and Baker drew from Bullock in making these points.

We hope that these examples will cause you to think about how you use your sources. Obviously no one expects you to come up with something that is entirely original and completely removed from what other people have said. The key is to acknowledge the ideas of others and to use the information they provide as the basis for your own comments. Generally, you don't need to give credit for anything that's common knowledge. For example, if you were discussing the receptive fields of neurons, you would not need to cite the original descriptions because the term is common currency in physiology and psychology. However, if you were discussing specific characteristics of receptive fields, then you would need to refer to your sources. Always document any fact or claim that is unfamiliar or open to question.

Don't be afraid that your work will seem weaker if you acknowledge the ideas of others. On the contrary, it will be all the more convincing: serious academic treatises are almost always built on the work of preceding scholars. If you are unsure whether you are relying too much on your sources, check with your instructor *before* you write your paper.

References

Broad, W., & Wade, N. (1982). *Betrayers of the truth*. New York: Simon and Schuster.

Spear, P.D., Penrod, S.D., & Baker, T.B. (1988). *Psychology: Perspectives on behavior*. New York: Wiley.

Note

[1]The following is based on a description of academic fraud and the honour system at the University of Virginia, but uses different examples.

4

Writing an essay or
research paper

Unlike students in the humanities, science students don't necessarily get practice in writing essays. It is not unusual for students in upper-level psychology courses to confess that they have not yet written an essay in university. If you are one of the many students who dread writing an academic essay or research paper, you will find that following a few simple steps in planning and organizing will make the task easier—and the result better.

There are many similarities between writing an essay in English or history and one in psychology or biology. There are also some differences. In particular, a scientific essay is usually a review of a body of literature, written to support a particular thesis or to outline what is known about a particular topic. The trick to writing a good scientific essay is to organize your material well and provide a good story line. Try to avoid the kind of paper that is nothing more than an annotated bibliography of the papers you have read: "Smith (1966) studied . . ."; "In 1973, Jones reported . . ."; "An interesting result was obtained by Griffiths & Wilson (1981)"; and so on. Such papers are not only tedious to read, but often difficult to follow. The solution to this problem is to begin with a well-organized outline and stick to it when you actually write the paper.

The planning stage

Some students claim they can write essays without any planning at all. On the rare occasions when they succeed, their writing is usually not as spontaneous as it seems: almost certainly, they have thought or talked a good deal about the subject in advance, and come to the task with some ready-made ideas. More often, trying to write a lengthy paper without planning just leads them to frustration. They get stuck in the middle and don't know how to finish, or suddenly realize that they are rambling off in the wrong direction.

In contrast, most writers say that the planning, or pre-writing, stage is the most important part of the whole process. Certainly the evidence shows that poor planning usually leads to disorganized writing; in the majority of students' papers the single greatest improvement would not be better research or better grammar, but better organization.

This insistence on planning doesn't rule out exploratory writing. Many people find that the act of writing itself is the best way to generate ideas or overcome writer's block; the hard decisions about organization come after they've put something down on the page. Whether you organize before or after you begin to write, though, at some point you need to plan.

Dealing with an assigned topic

If the topic of your essay is supplied by your instructor, you need to analyze it carefully; there are several key words that will tell you what you should be doing. You also need to make sure you don't neglect anything that is asked for. Distinguish the main focus from subordinate concerns. A common error in dealing with prescribed topics is to empha-size one portion while giving short shrift to another. Give each part its proper due—and make sure that you actually do what the instructions tell you to do. If you don't, you may receive a low grade, no matter how good your essay is. Some of the more common instructions are these:

outline   state simply, without much development of each point (unless asked).

trace   review by looking back—on stages or steps in a process, or on causes of an occurrence.

explain   show how or why something happens.

discuss   examine or analyze in an orderly way. This instruction allows you considerable freedom, as long as you take into account contrary evidence or ideas.

compare   examine differences as well as similarities. We discuss com-parisons in more detail on pp. 35-6.

evaluate   analyze strengths and weaknesses, providing an overall assessment of worth.

These and other verbs tell you how to approach your topic; be sure that you know what they mean—and follow them carefully.

Choosing a topic

Although you will sometimes be assigned a topic or asked to answer a specific question, for many papers you are limited only by the area covered in the course. "Cognitive development in children" or "the psychology of persuasion" are typical examples. In such cases you need to select a topic that you know you can deal with comfortably. Remember that the purpose of writing a paper is to help you learn about a topic, so it should not be one that is overly familiar to you. On the other hand, don't overextend yourself. Here are some guidelines:

- *Choose a topic that interests you.* Otherwise, you won't be able to work up much enthusiasm either for doing the research or for writing the paper.
- *Choose a topic on which sufficient material is readily available to you.* However fascinating a topic may be, if your library doesn't have the most important books or journals in that area, it's not a good idea to pursue it.
- *Do not choose a topic that is too difficult.* If you decide to write a paper that requires detailed knowledge of a specific field — whether brain physiology or statistics — be sure you have sufficient background, or you will not understand the literature.
- *Limit your topic to something manageable.* Beware of subject areas that are very broad: you don't want to put yourself in the position of having to deal with too much material.

Once you know the general topic you want to write about, the most successful strategy is to look for a logically distinct subtopic that will be manageable in the time and space available to you. For example, under the general topic of "neural plasticity" you would have an enormous number of potential paper topics. To narrow the field, you might begin by drawing a tree diagram of some of these possibilities, as illustrated in Figure 4.1.

Obviously, there are many more options than this, and some of the topic areas may overlap, but such a diagram can help you to narrow your choices down to a number you can comfortably handle.

Reading primary material

In Chapter 2 we discussed how you might go about finding the relevant references in your field. The next step is to start reading through some of those original papers. Primary material is the direct

Figure 4.1

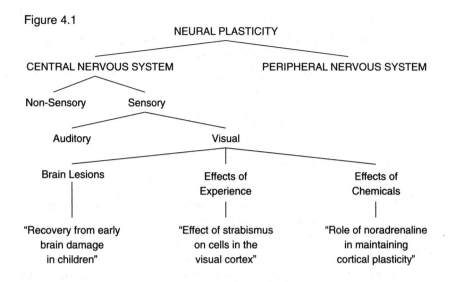

evidence—usually journal articles and sometimes books—on which you will base your own paper. Surprising as it may seem, the best way to begin working with this material is to give it a fast skim. Don't just start reading every article from beginning to end. Read the "Introduction" sections of several papers to get a sense of the kinds of questions that the authors are asking. Once you have an overview it will be easier to focus your own questions for a more directed and analytic second reading. Make no mistake: a superficial reading is not all you need. You will have to work through the material carefully a second time. But an initial skim followed by a focused second reading will give you a much more thorough understanding than one slow plod ever will.

A comment about secondary sources

In disciplines such as English or philosophy, where students have a good deal of freedom to express personal opinions, instructors may discourage secondary reading because they know that students who turn to commentaries may be so overwhelmed by the weight of authority that they produce trite, second-hand work. In the sciences, by contrast, your first task is to find out what is known about a particular topic. Under those circumstances, book chapters and review articles, provided they are used judiciously, can be a good way of getting a quick overview of your topic. Secondary sources can never substitute for your own active reading of the primary material, but they can serve a useful purpose.

Organizing your material

Once you have started collecting materials for your paper, you need to organize it in some way. There are four important things you need to do: (1) keep track of where your information comes from; (2) collect information on different aspects of your topic; (3) decide on the approach you will take; and (4) arrange information into an order that you can follow when you begin to write. For the first two, the easiest strategy is to use an index-card system; for the third and fourth, you need to develop a theme or a thesis and create an outline.

Keeping track. Nothing is more frustrating than to find that you aren't sure where a piece of information came from. Each time you read an article or a book chapter, write down the reference on an index card. This is important in case you want to find that reference again, and/or list it in your completed paper. It may be helpful also to put down the library call number. Write the full reference in the format that you will use for your reference list (see Chapter 8); then, as you accumulate more references, sort them into alphabetical order. When the time comes to prepare your *Reference* section you can simply type them in from the cards. An added advantage of this system is that you can start to build up a database of references that may come in handy for other papers on similar topics. Another useful strategy for your reference cards is to put down two or three key words that may help to remind you what the article was about.

Collecting information. Finding your research material is one thing; making sure that you have correctly summarized what you have read is another. You must take notes that are dependable and easy to use. With time you will develop your own best method, but here again, the index-card system works well. Using a different set of index cards from the ones containing the full reference, write down the short citation (e.g., Smith & Smith, 1993) so that you can cross-refer to your other cards. Then, below the citation, note the major points of the article. You don't need to go into much detail—just enough to help you remember what the paper was about. (You can always go back if you need more detail.) It's also worthwhile to jot down a reminder of how you felt about the paper. Then when you're doing your final write-up and you see "useful review," you might want to go back and read it over again; but if it was "incomprehensible," or too "theoretical," you might decide to skip that particular paper.

An alternative to using cards for individual sources, especially if you're familiar with the major issues you will be discussing, is to let each card deal with a specific topic. In this case, you would indicate the topic and source at the top of each card and then make your notes. If a single paper deals with several different aspects of your subject, you would use several different cards. The advantage of this system is that, once you have generated an outline, it's easy to sort your material for writing.

Deciding on an approach. If your assignment is simply to write an essay on a particular topic, then it is up to you to decide how you will approach it. You need a central, controlling idea that will lead the reader through the paper. At all costs you want to avoid having the reader ask, "What is the point that this paper is trying to make?"

There are two general approaches you can take. The first is to organize your essay around a theme that will serve to hold together your information and ideas as you write. A good strategy is to write a single-phrase statement of your theme to serve as an anchor before you begin writing: for example, "Factors that determine performance on intelligence tests," or "The development of speech perception in infants." This phrase will become the title of your final paper. Having defined your topic in this way, you can then go on to review and discuss different aspects of it. You are not necessarily taking a point of view; rather, you are providing the reader with a summary of the available literature.

An alternative approach, which many students prefer, is to develop and defend a particular thesis. The argumentative form is perhaps easier to organize and more likely to produce forceful writing. This approach certainly makes for a more interesting essay if it is done well. For example, if you were writing on intelligence, you might take the position that cultural bias invalidates the results of many intelligence tests. Or you could argue that intellectual ability is inherited, and that IQ tests are the most valid measurements we have. It doesn't really matter what position you take, as you long as you make a convincing case for it.

The next step is to select a single theme or thesis as the focal point around which you will organize your material. Although you may start with a particular "working thesis," it doesn't have to be the final one; sometimes you will change your opinion as you work your way through the literature. A working thesis simply serves as a linchpin, holding together your information and ideas as you organize. At some point in the writing process you will probably want to make your working thesis into an explicit statement that can appear in your introduction. But even if you don't state it formally, using a working thesis will help you define your intentions, make your research more selective, and focus your essay.

In developing your thesis there are three rules to follow: make it limited, make it unified, and make it exact (see McCrimmon, 1976).

Make it limited. A limited thesis is one that is narrow enough to be workable. Suppose, for example, that your general subject is sexuality and adolescence. Such a subject is much too broad to be dealt with in an essay of two or three thousand words; you must limit it in some way and create a line of argument for which you can provide adequate supporting evidence. For example, you might want to discuss factors that influence contraceptive use, or the role of TV and movies in setting models for sexual behaviour and attitudes.

Make it unified. To be unified, your thesis must have one controlling idea. Beware of the double-headed thesis. In the example above, about adolescent sexuality, a thesis could be: "Sexual attitudes in the 1960s were permissive because children were rebelling against their conservative parents, but now attitudes are more conservative because of concerns about AIDS." What is the controlling idea here? Is it parent-child relationships, or the way that external threats can influence behaviour? It is possible to have two or more related ideas in a thesis, but only if one of them is clearly in control, with all the other ideas subordinate to it: "Although it has been argued that studies of operant conditioning are not very useful, the principles developed from them are applied in many real-life situations."

Make it exact. It is important, especially when you are defending a position, to avoid vague terms such as "interesting" and "significant," as in "Banting and Best's early failures were significant steps towards their discovery of insulin." Were the failures significant because they provided an incentive to work harder, or because they provided insights that could be used later? Remember to be as specific as possible in creating your thesis, in order to focus your essay. Don't just make an assertion—give the main reasons for it. Instead of saying simply "Intensive planting practices can increase crop yields substantially" and leaving it at that, add an explanation: ". . . because the plants are positioned strategically to allow maximum use of the space available and the leaf cover provides a living mulch that discourages the growth of weeds."

Creating an outline

Individual writers differ in their need for a formal plan. Some say they never construct an outline, and others maintain they can't write without one; most fall somewhere in between. Because organization is such a common problem, though, it's a good idea to know how to draw up an effective plan.

If you have special problems with organizing material, your outline should be formal, in complete sentences. On the other hand, if your mind is naturally logical, you may find it's enough just to jot down a few words on a scrap of paper. For most students, an informal but well-organized outline in point form is the most useful.

If you have organized your library research materials on topic cards, these can provide a simple way to begin your outline. Rearranging the cards in different orders will give you an idea of how topics fit together before you put the outline down on paper.

Nowadays, a more sophisticated approach is to use your word processor. Most of the major word-processing packages will allow you to create an outline automatically, with major headings and subheadings. You can move subtopics around from one heading to another, or change main headings to subheadings, and vice versa. A useful strategy is to begin the outline with single keywords and then gradually expand it into topics and, eventually, complete sentences. With some thought, you can construct your whole paper within the framework of the outline.

When you are constructing an outline, there are several points to keep in mind. Suppose you were writing a paper on biological navigation:

Thesis: Refined navigational skills are found in many different species, but they serve quite different purposes.

I. Orienting and navigating seen in many different kinds of animal.
  A. Birds
    1. Arctic tern
    2. Homing pigeon
  B. Insects
    1. Army ant
    2. Monarch butterfly
  C. Fish
    1. Salmon

II. Different animals use different cues.
  A. Celestial cues
    1. Sun-compass
    2. Star navigation

    B. Terrestrial cues
        1. Geomagnetism
        2. Barometric pressure
        3. Odour trails
        4. Landmarks

    III. Navigating serves different purposes
        A. Migration
            1. Favourable climate
            2. Food availability
            3. Breeding grounds
        B. Locating local food sources
            1. Honeybee
            2. Ant

The guidelines for this kind of outline are simple:

Arrange your outline according to themes. In the example above, there are three main themes: a description of the range of animals that navigate, the cues they use, and the reasons they navigate. Your first section could be quite short, simply giving examples of navigational feats in different species. Then in the second and third sections you would focus on cues and reasons, again using different species as examples. Arranging your material according to themes will produce a much more readable essay than, say, simply listing various animals and explaining why they navigate and what cues they use.

Code your categories. Use different sets of markings to establish the relative importance of your entries. The example here moves from roman numerals to letters to arabic numbers, but you could use another system. Most outlining programs will provide a coding system automatically.

Categorize according to importance. Make sure that only items of equal value are put in equivalent categories. Give major points more weight than minor ones.

Check lines of connection. Make sure that each of the main categories is directly linked to the central thesis; then see that each subcategory is directly linked to the larger category that contains it.

Be consistent. In arranging your points, be consistent. You may choose to move either from the most important point to the least important, or vice versa, as long as you follow the same order each time.

One final word: be prepared to change your outline at any time in the writing process. An outline is not meant to put an iron clamp on your thinking, but to relieve anxiety about where you're heading. A careful outline prevents frustration and dead ends—that "I'm stuck, where can I go from here?" feeling. But since the very act of writing will usually generate new ideas, you should be ready to modify your original plan. Just remember that any new outline must have the consistency and clear connections required for a unified essay.

The writing stage

Writing the first draft

Rather than labour for excellence from scratch, most writers find it easiest to write the first draft as quickly as possible and then do extensive revisions later. However you begin, you can't expect the first draft to be the final copy. Skilled writers know that revising is a necessary part of the writing process, and that the care taken with revisions makes the difference between a mediocre essay and a good one.

You don't need to write all parts of the essay in the same order in which they are to appear in the final copy. In fact, many students find the introduction the hardest part to write. If you face the first blank page with a growing sense of paralysis, try leaving the introduction until later, and start with the first idea in your outline. If you feel so intimidated that you haven't even been able to draw up an outline, you might try John Trimble's approach and charge right ahead with any kind of beginning—even a simple "My first thoughts on this subject are . . ." (Trimble, 1975). Instead of sharpening pencils or running out for a snack, try to get going. Don't worry about grammar or wording; scratch out pages or throw them away if you must. Remember, the object is to get your writing juices flowing.

Of course, you can't expect this kind of exploratory writing to resemble the first draft that follows an outline. You will probably need to do a great deal more changing and reorganizing, but at least you will have the relief of seeing words on a page to work with. Many experienced writers—and not only those with writer's block—find this the most productive way to proceed.

Developing your ideas: some common patterns

The way you develop your ideas will depend on your topic, and topics can vary enormously. Even so, most research papers follow one of a few basic organizational patterns. Here's how to use each pattern effectively.

Defining

Sometimes a whole paper is an extended definition, explaining the meaning of a concept that is complicated, controversial, or simply important to your field of study: for example, the *Superego* in psycho-analytic writings, *prions* in microbiology, or *evolution* in biology. More often, perhaps, you may want to begin a detailed discussion of a topic by defining a key term, and then shift to a different organizational pattern. In either case, make your definition exact. It should be broad enough to include all the things that belong in the category and at the same time narrow enough to exclude things that don't belong. A good definition builds a kind of verbal fence around a word, herding together all the members of the class and cutting off all outsiders.

For any discussion of a term that goes beyond a bare definition, of course, you should give concrete illustrations or examples; depending on the nature of your paper, these could vary in length from one or two sentences to several paragraphs or even pages. If you were defining the Superego, for instance, you would probably want to discuss at some length the theories of leading psychoanalysts.

In an extended definition, it's also useful to point out the differences between the term in question and other terms that may be connected or perhaps confused with it. For instance, if you were defining prions you might want to distinguish them from viruses; if you were defining a modern version of evolutionary theory, you should contrast it with classic Darwinian theory.

Classifying

Classifying means dividing something into its separate parts according to some principle of selection. The principle or criterion may vary; you could classify crops, for example, according to how they grow (above the ground or below the ground), how long they take to mature, or what climatic conditions they require; the population of an ecological niche might be classified according to species present, distribution within the niche, degree of interdependence, and so on. If you are organizing your essay by a system of classification, remember the following:

- All members of a class must be accounted for. If any are left over, you need to alter some categories or add more.
- Categories can be divided into subcategories. You should consider using subcategories if there are significant differences within a category. For instance, if you were classifying the effects of brain damage according to the site of the lesion, you might want to create subcategories according to memory deficits, language problems, perceptual difficulties, and so on.
- Any subcategory should contain at least two items.

Explaining a process

This kind of organization shows how something works or has worked, whether it be the weather cycle, the photochemical reactions of the eye, or the mechanisms of hibernation. The important point to remember is to be systematic, to break down the process into a series of steps or stages. Although your order will vary depending on circumstances, most often it will be chronological, in which case you should see that the sequence is accurate and easy to follow. Whatever the arrangement, you can generally make the process easier to follow if you start a new paragraph for each new stage.

Tracing causes and effects

A cause-and-effect analysis is really a particular kind of process discussion, in which certain events are shown to have led to or resulted from other events. Usually you are explaining why something happened. The main warning here is to avoid over-simplifying. If you are tracing causes, distinguish between a direct cause and a contributing cause, between what is a condition of something happening and what is merely a correlation or coincidence. For example, if you discover that there is a high correlation between the number of garbage dumps and the number of polar bears sighted around Churchill, Manitoba, you should not conclude that the bears breed in the garbage dumps. Similarly, you must be sure that the result you mention is a genuine product of the event or action.

Comparing

Many successful essays are based on comparisons. Even if it is not specifically part of your assignment, by choosing a limited number of items to compare—theories, neural mechanisms, factors that might influence behaviour, or whatever—you can create a clear focus for your paper. Just be sure that you deal with differences as well as similarities.

When you prepare your outline for this kind of paper, it is important to decide how you will set up your comparisons. The easiest method, though not always the best, is to discuss the first subject in the comparison thoroughly and then move on to the second. The problem with this kind of comparison is that it often sounds like two separate essays slapped together. To be successful you must integrate the two subjects, first in your introduction (by putting them both in a single context) and again in your conclusion, where you should bring together the important points you have made about each. When discussing the second subject, you should always refer back to your discussion of your first subject. This method may be the wisest choice if the subjects for comparison seem so unlike that it is hard to create similar categories in which to place them for discussion—if the points you are making about X are of a different type from the points you are making about Y.

If it is possible to find similar criteria or categories for discussing both subjects, however, the comparison will be more effective if you organize it so that you make comparisons within one category before moving on to the next. Because this kind of comparison is more tightly integrated, the reader can more readily see the similarities and differences between the subjects. As a result, the essay is likely to be more forceful.

Introductions

The beginning of a research paper has a dual purpose: to indicate both the topic and your approach to it, and to whet your reader's appetite for what you have to say. One effective way of introducing a topic is to place it in a context—to supply a kind of backdrop that will put it in perspective. You step back a pace and discuss the area into which your topic fits, and then gradually lead into your specific field of discussion. Baker (1981) calls this the funnel approach. For example, suppose that your topic is the specific action of certain neurotoxins on the nervous system. You might begin with a more general discussion of the effects of some of the naturally occurring neurotoxins, such as the one produced by the puffer fish. The funnel opening is applicable to almost any kind of paper.

You want to catch your reader's interest right from the start—you know from your own reading how a dull beginning can put you off. But it's important that your lead-in relate to your topic: never sacrifice relevance for catchiness. Finally, whether your introduction is one paragraph or several, make sure that by the end of it your reader clearly knows the direction you are taking.

Conclusions

Endings can be painful—sometimes for the reader as much as for the writer. Too often, the feeling that one ought to say something profound and memorable produces either a pompous or a meaningless ending. You know the sort of thing:

> This is not to say that the research of the last decade has been in vain, to the contrary, we have learned a tremendous amount. Critical and conflicting evidence does tell us however, that we still have a long way to go before we can deal in absolutes (*student essay, 1985*).

Even if you ignore the grammatical difficulties in this example, it's easy to see that these two sentences might better have been omitted. Experienced editors often say that many articles and essays would be better without their final paragraphs: in other words, when you have finished saying what you want to say, the only thing to do is stop. This advice works best for short papers where you need to keep the central point firmly in the foreground and don't need to remind the reader of it. However, for longer pieces, where you have developed a number of ideas or a complex line of argument, you should provide a sense of closure. Readers welcome an ending that helps to tie the ideas together; they don't like to feel they've been left dangling. And since the final impression is often the most lasting, it's in your interest to finish strongly. Simply restating your thesis or summarizing what you have already said isn't forceful enough. You need to add something more.

One successful strategy is what Baker (1981) calls the inverse funnel approach, as opposed to the funnel approach of the opening paragraph. In this model, your conclusion restates the thesis in different words and then discusses its implications. The only danger in moving to a wider perspective is that you may try to embrace too much. When a conclusion expands too far it tends to lose focus, as in the example above. It's always better to discuss specific implications than to trail off with vague generalities.

The editing stage

Often the best writer in a class is not the one who can dash off a fluent first draft, but the one who is the best editor. To edit your work well you need to see it as the reader will; you have to distinguish between what you meant to say and what is actually on the page. For this reason it's a good idea to leave some time between drafts so that when you begin to edit you will be looking at the writing afresh, rather than reviewing it from memory. Now's the time to go to a movie or do something that will take your mind off your work. Without this distancing period you can become so involved that it's hard to see your paper objectively.

Editing doesn't mean simply checking your work for errors in grammar or spelling. It means looking at the piece as a whole to see if the ideas are (1) well organized, (2) well documented, and (3) well expressed. It may mean adding some paragraphs, deleting others, and shifting still others around. It very likely means adding, deleting, and shifting sentences and phrases. Experienced writers may be able to check several aspects of their work at the same time, but if you are inexperienced or in doubt about your writing, it's best to look at the organization of the ideas before you tackle sentence structure, diction, style, and documentation. Ask yourself, as you read through your paper, whether it flows properly: is the rhythm of your reading comfortable, or do some passages slow you down because they're awkwardly constructed? Such problems can often be corrected just by shuffling the word order a little.

What follows is a check-list of questions to ask yourself as you begin editing. Far from being all-inclusive, it focuses on the first step: examining the organization. You probably won't want to check through your work separately for each question: you can group some together and overlook others, depending on your own strengths and weaknesses as a writer.

Preliminary editing check-list

1. Are the purpose and approach of this essay evident from the beginning?

2. Are all sections of the paper relevant to the topic?

3. Is the organization logical?

4. Are the ideas sufficiently developed? Is there enough evidence, explanation, and illustration?

5. Would an educated person who hasn't read the primary material understand everything I'm saying? Should I clarify some parts or add any explanatory material?

6. In presenting my argument, do I take into account opposing arguments or evidence?

7. Do my paragraph divisions give coherence to my ideas? Do I use them to cluster similar ideas and signal changes of ideas?

8. Do any parts of the paper seem disjointed? Should I add more transitional words or logical indicators to make the sequence of ideas easier to follow?

Another approach would be to devise your own check-list based on the faults of previous assignments. This is particularly useful when you move from the overview to the close focus on sentence structure, diction, punctuation, spelling, and style. If you have a particular weak area—for example, irrelevant evidence, faulty logic, or run-on sentences—you should give it special attention. Keeping a personal check-list will save you from repeating the same old mistakes.

A note on word-processors

Although the most important part of a paper is its content, it is always to your advantage to make sure that the final version of your paper is as neat as possible. A well-typed, visually appealing essay creates a receptive reader and, fairly or unfairly, often gets a higher mark than a handwritten one—especially if the handwriting is messy or hard to read. Nowadays, almost all students have access to a word-processor when they come to write their papers. This makes it much easier to produce an elegant piece of work.

Using a word-processor simplifies many of the tasks of writing: you can correct mistakes before they arrive on paper, check your spelling, rearrange your material for ease of reading, and print out a neat and tidy final copy. Most systems are easy to learn and they can speed up your writing considerably, especially if you use the word-processor to generate the outline that you expand into your paper. To some extent they can also help you to improve your writing skills, because they make it easier for you to read what you have written and decide whether it is worth keeping. If you are already comfortable with word-processors, you probably don't need the following advice. For those who are just starting to use them, though, here's a basic introduction.

1. Type your material directly into the computer. The traditional way of writing a paper that eventually will be typed is to write it out in longhand, and then type it or have someone else type it for you. You can speed up the physical writing process enormously by typing your paper directly into the computer. Even if you aren't an expert typist, the time spent thinking will far outweigh the time it takes to enter the words into the computer. A common argument against writing in this fashion is "I can't think at the typewriter," but give it a try anyway. You'll probably find that it's easier to keep going when you can see your thoughts appearing in a legible form in front of you.

2. Try different ways of organizing your paper. Although your outline should determine the overall structure of your paper, sometimes you may want to look to see how it flows, paragraph by paragraph. One of the most useful aspects of a word-processing system is that it allows you to move blocks of text around so that you can try out different ways of organizing your material. If you've ever reached the point where your handwritten version has become so complicated that you have to copy the whole thing out again to make any sense of it, you will appreciate being able to make on-screen corrections and rearrangements. You can try out a whole new organizational structure, read it through—and if you don't like it, go back to your original version.

3. Don't let the system rule your thinking. Seeing something typed out neatly on a screen or on paper makes it look more acceptable than messy handwriting, even though the quality of the work may be no different. Don't be fooled into thinking that quality typing replaces quality thinking. Read over your work with a critical eye, in the knowledge that you can easily change something that is unsatisfactory. The word-processor is a tool for you to use, no more than that.

4. Save regularly and back up your files. If you are used to working with a computer you know the importance of this advice; if not, then take it to heart. There is nothing more agonizing than to discover that something has gone wrong and caused you to lose everything you've been working on for hours. It doesn't happen very often, but it happens at least once to everyone, and always unexpectedly. This problem is simple to avoid. When you are actually writing, save your work file every 15 minutes or so (or set your word-processor to do this automatically). Then when your room-mate pulls the plug on the computer to turn on the TV, the most you will lose is whatever you've done since the last time you saved your file. A potentially more serious problem will arise if your hard disk becomes damaged, so that you lose your whole file. To avoid even the faintest possibility of such a loss, always save a copy of your file onto a floppy disk and keep it in some safe place, away from the computer. Instructors are not always sympathetic to excuse that you "lost the paper on the computer" when you submit an essay late.

You should also be sure to keep your computer file at least until your paper has been submitted and marked. We are aware of several cases of alleged plagiarism whose resolution depended on whether the student could produce a disk version of the paper.

If you don't have access to a word-processor or typewriter, take special care that your script is neat and easy to read. If your handwriting is poor, print instead. Finally, however you write your paper, always double-space your lines and leave wide margins on sides, top, and bottom, framing the script in white. Leave at least three centimetres at least at the sides and top and four centimetres at the bottom, so that the reader has ample space to write comments. Number each page at the top right-hand corner, and provide a neat, well-spaced cover page including the title, your name, your instructor's name, and the number of your course. Good looks won't substitute for good thinking, but they will certainly enhance it.

References

Baker, S. (1981). *The practical stylist* (5th ed.). New York: Harper & Row.

McCrimmon, J. (1976). *Writing with a purpose* (6th ed.). Boston: Houghton Mifflin.

Trimble, J.R. (1975). *Writing with style: Conversations on the art of writing*. Englewood Cliffs, NJ: Prentice-Hall.

5

Writing a lab report I:

Organization and format

If you are studying psychology or biological sciences, much of the writing you do will take the form of lab reports: that is, formal descriptions of experiments you have done.

Writing a lab report is a little different from writing an English essay. Scientists are interested in the orderly presentation of factual evidence to support hypotheses or theories. This means that the structure of reports in the sciences will tend to be more formal than in non-science disciplines. It also means that you must be objective in the way you report your data. Although you may wish to make a case for a particular hypothesis, it's essential to separate the data themselves from your own speculations about them. You must present your information so that anyone who reads your report can understand clearly what you've done in your experiment. On the basis of the evidence you present, the reader should be free to draw his or her own conclusions. If you've done a good job, they will be the same as yours.

Purpose and reader

Whether you are writing for a prestigious journal or for a graduate-student lab instructor, you goal is to disseminate scientific information. This means that you cannot take your reader's knowledge for granted. As an undergraduate, you will be writing lab reports to describe studies you have conducted. You will also be trying to show that you understand a particular phenomenon or theory. As is the case in professional scientific writing, you can assume that the reader—your instructor—is familiar with basic scientific terms, so you won't need to define or explain them. However, you cannot assume that your instructor is omniscient. He or she will be frustrated to be told that "The subjects' settings were read directly from the micrometer drive" if this is the first time a micrometer has been mentioned anywhere in the paper. Be sure, then, that you have mentioned pieces of equipment or procedures before you start making casual references to them. You can also assume that your reader will be on the lookout for any weaknesses in methodology or analysis, and any omissions of important data.

Lab reports and Honours theses

In a typical lab course you will be assigned several experiments to carry out and write up. Occasionally you may get a chance to do an independent project, but most of the time you will be working under pretty close supervision. As you progress through your university career, however, you will be required to do more independent work, sometimes including an Honours thesis. In their final format, lab reports and theses are quite similar, and the rules we describe later in the chapter apply to both. But, the thesis is a much bigger project, and it requires a good deal more preparation.

Although the primary purpose of this book is to help you express yourself well in writing, it's important to keep in mind that what you finally write is largely a product of what you have done before you get to the writing stage. Since, in the case of an Honours thesis, you will be spending virtually a whole academic year preparing to write a single paper, it is all the more important that you think about how you'll proceed. It's surprising, but some students do not have a clear idea of what is required for an Honours thesis until they have actually begun work on it, and in some cases until they have been working on it for quite a while. This section will give you a brief overview of what is required to prepare for an Honours thesis that involves an empirical research project. Knowing what is expected of you from the beginning should make it much easier to write up a final paper that will earn you a good mark.

What is an Honours thesis?

An Honours thesis is an opportunity for you to demonstrate that you are capable of carrying out independent scientific research (albeit with some guidance from your adviser) and presenting it in the form of a paper. It is equally important, however, to be aware of what a thesis is *not*. First, it is not primarily intended to be an original and significant contribution to the literature of your discipline. Although many theses are excellent pieces of work, and some of the best do get published, this is not the reason for doing the work. You must not assume that you have to create a masterpiece and solve a "big" problem in your discipline. We have seen many students get bogged down after designing a complicated experiment that required them to test dozens of subjects; as a result, they ran out of time and could not do a good job on their data analysis or write-up. Research is time-consuming, and it often involves many false starts. When you are doing a thesis over the course of a single year, you don't have the flexibility to go back and start again if things don't work out. For this reason it's essential to set reasonable goals and choose a project that will be manageable. You can demonstrate your research skills just as well—sometimes better—with a simple project as with a complicated one.

You should also be aware that the subject area in which you choose to do your thesis is less important than you might think. For example, many students in psychology who aspire to go on to graduate programs in clinical psychology naturally want to do their theses in this area. But in fact clinical psychology is one of the most difficult areas in which to do meaningful research in a short period of time. It may be difficult to get ethics clearance; the potential subject population may not be readily available; and the rules of confidentiality may prevent a student from gathering important data. You can produce an excellent thesis in an area such as clinical psychology (with the right adviser and a carefully chosen project), but you may have to work a lot harder than, say, a student doing a cognitive psychology thesis. Similarly, students who do animal research often find that although the project is straightforward, they have to commit themselves to many hours of testing, often over weekends and holidays.

The important thing is to choose a feasible project that you will find interesting. If you keep this in mind, the tasks of selecting a topic and running the study will be much easier.

Differences between a lab report and a thesis

The main differences between a lab report and a thesis are the amount of background that you will be expected to provide in your *Introduction*, the scale of your study, and the extent of your *Discussion* section. Otherwise, the final write-up should follow a similar format. One advantage in writing the thesis is that you will often have the chance to submit preliminary drafts to your adviser for comments before you write the final version. Remember, though, that to get feedback you have to submit the drafts in time for someone to read them. Don't leave everything until the last minute!

The structure of a lab report

Although the general format of lab reports is similar for all disciplines, formal style requirements vary considerably. Your lab instructor will give you the specific information for your discipline. In addition, however, you can obtain a lot of information about both style and format from the *Publication Manual of the American Psychological Association* (American Psychological Association, 1994) and the *CBE Style Manual*, published by the Council of Biology Editors (1983). The *CBE Style Manual* is most useful for those working in disciplines where it is important to be accurate when describing different species of plants or animals or different chemical compounds. Most of the suggestions that follow are adapted from the *APA Manual*, and we refer you there for more details.

Because the information in scientific reports must be easy for the reader to find and assess, it should be organized into separate sections, each with a heading. By convention, most lab reports follow a standard order:

1. Title page
2. Abstract
3. Introduction
4. Method (may include some or all of the following subsections: Subjects or Participants, Materials, Apparatus, Design, Procedure)
5. Results (including figures and tables)
6. Discussion
7. References

The order of these sections is always the same; however, some sections may be combined, or have slightly different names, depending how much information you have in each one. Different disciplines also have slightly different rules, but the following will give you an overview of what should go into each section of your report.

Title page

The first page of your report is always the title page. It should include the title of the paper, your name (and perhaps your student number), the name of the course and the instructor, and the date of submission. Your title should be brief—about 10 or 12 words—but informative, clearly indicating the topic and scope of your study. Use words in the title that would be useful if you were doing a literature search for studies on your topic. Avoid meaningless phrases, such as "A Study of . . ." or "Observations on . . ."; simply state what it is that you are studying: for example, "Effects of Gamma Rays on Growth Rate of Man-in-the-Moon Marigolds."

Abstract

The *Abstract* appears on a separate page following the title page. This brief, comprehensive summary of your report should be able to stand alone; that is, someone should be able to read it and know exactly what the experiment was about, what the results were, and how you interpreted them. For a professional researcher, the abstract is arguably the most important section of a paper because it is the first point of access in a literature search. If the abstract does not pique the reader's interest, the whole report is likely to be ignored. For this reason it should include all the major points of your study — and exclude anything that is not in the report itself. Using no more than roughly 120 words, it should describe the purpose of the experiment, the participants, the experimental apparatus or materials, the procedure, the main results, including statistical significance levels, and your conclusions. With the word-number restrictions, you don't have space to be vague. Instead of saying "The purpose of the experiments in this study was . . .", say "I studied. . . ." And at the end, rather than state the obvious — for example, "The results of this study are discussed" — state directly what your conclusions are: "The results demonstrate that . . ." or "I conclude that . . ."

Introduction

The *Introduction* describes the problem you are studying, the rationale for studying it, and the research strategy you will use to obtain the relevant data. This is also where you will present your experimental hypothesis and a statement either of what you expect to find or of the question you plan to examine. Not all experiments make explicit predictions; sometimes you may simply be asking a question: for example, if you were interested in the social development of young infants, you might ask about the age of a baby's first smile and how the frequency of social smiling changed with age. But even if you don't make a specific prediction, you should state your question clearly.

You should also explain the background to your problem in the form of a brief historical review of the relevant literature. This should not be an exhaustive discussion, but rather an overview that serves to recognize the prior work of others and to show how your own study relates to what has come before. You don't need to summarize all the aspects of the studies you cite, only those points that are relevant to your own study, including, if appropriate, the theory underlying your own experiment. If, as is often the case, the purpose is to test a hypothesis about a specific problem, you should state clearly both the nature of the problem and what you expect to find.

The final paragraph or so of your *Introduction* should be a summary of what you did in your experiment. It should include a description of the variables that you manipulated, a formal statement of your experimental hypotheses, and a brief explanation of the reasons why you expected to get a particular pattern of results.

Method

The *Method* section is usually made up of several labelled subsections. These describe the organisms you were working with, your experimental apparatus and materials, and your procedure.

Subjects/Participants. Whether in psychology or in other disciplines in which the experiment has been carried out using live organisms, you need a section describing your experimental animal. If these animals happen to be human, you need to give any information about them that is relevant to the experiment. This is important because the extent to which you can generalize your results depends on how representative your sample is of a population. For example, if you were studying people's judgements of the meanings of certain kinds of words, you would need to mention whether or not all the participants were native English speakers. Typically, you would give also the average age of the group and their status ("university undergraduates" or "3-year-old children registered in a pre-school program"). Your rule about what information to include should be "Is it relevant to the purpose of the study?" When you use non-human subjects, you should mention the species or strain and any special characteristics that they might possess. APA style recommends the term *participants* when using humans.

Apparatus/Materials. Depending on the discipline and the kind of experiment you are doing, this section may be entitled either *Apparatus* or *Materials*; consult with your instructor to find out the rules that apply to your own experiment. The *Materials* section should contain a description of the materials you used—for instance, chemicals or psychological test batteries. It should also provide a description of any experimental apparatus you used. You should describe all the essential components of any major pieces of equipment and how they were set up. If different arrangements of equipment were required, give a full list of the equipment in this section, and then in the *Procedure* section describe each separate arrangement before describing the respective procedures. If the equipment was a standard, commercially available item, it is customary to give the manufacturer's name and the model number. For example, if your psychology experiment required you to present patterns on the face of an oscilloscope cathode ray tube, you should say that they were "presented on a Tektronix 608 display monitor with a P31 phosphor," or whatever it was that you used.

Design. Sometimes, especially if your study involves a fairly complex experimental design, it is helpful to include a brief formal description of that design. This should include (1) a description of your independent and dependent variables, indicating which are between- and which are within-subject variables; (2) the composition of your experimental and control groups, and how the subjects were assigned to the groups; and (3) the statistical model: for example, a two-way factorial, or a repeated measures design.

Procedure. This section is a step-by-step description of how you carried out the experiment. If you have undertaken a number of tests, you should begin with a short summary statement listing the tests so that the reader will be prepared for the series. To avoid confusion, use the same order to describe the tests as you did to list them.

The *Procedure* section must be written with enough detail that others would have no difficulty in repeating the experiment in all its essential details. However, you should avoid any detail that is not directly relevant to the study. If you were measuring the effectiveness of different antibiotics on bacterial growth, you would have to describe the medium on which you grew the bacteria, the incubation temperature, the strength and amount of antibiotic given, and so on; you would not need to mention the fact that the experiment was carried out on the fifth floor of the Biology building.

If you are following instructions in a lab manual, you may not need to copy them out word for word; simply refer to the instructions and give details of any differences in your experiment.

Results

When professional scientists come across a new paper, they will read the *Abstract* first. After that they may only glance at the *Introduction* and *Methods*, then concentrate on the *Results* section, because this is where they will find the essence of the paper. In a sense, all the other sections of a lab report are subordinate to the *Results*. It is here that the readers will obtain their most important information. They may have questions about the methodology, and they may disagree with the interpretation presented in the *Discussion*, but they should be able to make their own evaluation of the findings on the basis of a *Results* section that presents the data clearly and unambiguously. For this reason, you should spend some time thinking about the best way to present your results. You have a lot of choices, and some ways are much better than others.

The *Results* section should contain a summary of all the data you collected, with sufficient detail to justify your conclusions. Typically, you will not provide individual subject data, but statistical summaries of your results. You might include some results in tabular form and others in figures. In writing the *Results* section, you should present all of your data, whether or not it supports your hypothesis. Although this is not the place to discuss the implications of your data, it is appropriate to guide your reader through the results. So, for example, you might say: "The first question was whether listening to loud music on a personal stereo impaired performance in a word search task. The average time taken . . . (description of your data and statistical analyses). . . . These results are consistent with the experimental hypothesis." Without discussing why the results turned out the way they did, you have provided the reader with a context in which to place the data you describe. This makes for much easier reading than a dry listing of means and statistical tests without any explanation.

Because the *Results* section is so important, the following chapter is devoted to the more technical aspects of presenting your data.

Discussion

This part of the lab report allows you the greatest freedom, because it permits you to examine and interpret the results and to comment on their significance. You want to show how the experiment produced its outcome, whether expected or unexpected, and to discuss those elements that influenced the results.

Before beginning your actual discussion, you should give a brief overview of the major findings of your study: for example, "The results of the present study demonstrated that university students could remember the details of lectures much better if they spent fifteen minutes organizing and expanding their lecture notes at the end of each class." The rest of the discussion would deal with the reasons why this might be so.

To help you decide what to include in the *Discussion* section, you might try to answer the following questions:

- Do the results reflect the objectives of the experiment?
- Do the results obtained agree with previous results as reported in the literature on the subject? If not, how can you account for the discrepancy between your own results and those published in the literature? What, if anything, may have gone wrong during your experiment, and why? What was the source of any error?
- Could the results have another explanation?
- Did the procedures you used help you to accomplish the purpose of the experiment? Does your experience in this experiment suggest a better way for next time?

The order of topics in your *Discussion* should be the same as that in your *Results*: discuss each of your findings in turn as you reported them in that section. If you have a result that you don't know how to explain, say so; never ignore an inconvenient finding in the hope that your instructor might not notice. A good *Discussion* section may not be able to tie up all the loose ends, but it must acknowledge that they are there.

You should always end with a statement of the conclusions that may be drawn from the experiment. Sometimes the conclusions are put in a separate section, but typically they form the final paragraph at the end of the *Discussion*. In the example above you might end by saying: "The findings of the present study suggest that if students were able to take a little extra time going over their notes at the end of each class, it is likely that they could improve their grades."

Sometimes, especially if the discussion is going to be straightforward, you can combine the *Results* and *Discussion* sections. In this case, the best strategy is to present each result, followed by a brief discussion. At the end, you should try to pull it all together in a concluding paragraph.

References

We have already discussed plagiarism in Chapter 3. The way to avoid even the suspicion of plagiarism is to support every non-original statement with a reference citation. Always refer to your sources unless the information you are providing is considered to be common knowledge. Each time you refer to a book or an article in the text of your report, cite the reference; then at the end of the paper make a list of all the sources you have cited. The precise form of the citations and reference list varies between disciplines; for more detail, see Chapter 8.

Footnotes

You should use footnotes as little as possible. If they are unavoidable, indicate where each one should go in the text by placing a number as a superscript at the point of insertion. At the back of the paper, after the references, list the footnotes in order, numbering them so that they correspond to the numbers you have used in the text.

References

American Psychological Association. (1994). *Publication manual of the American Psychological Association*. (4th ed.). Washington, DC: Author.

Council of Biological Editors. (1983). *CBE style manual. A guide for authors, editors, and publishers in the biological sciences*. (5th ed.). Bethesda, MD: Author.

6

Writing a lab report II:

Presentation of data

As we noted in the previous chapter, the *Results* section is the heart of
an experimental paper. If you don't present your results clearly, the lab
report isn't worth reading. Once you have gathered a set of data, you
must first analyze them and then decide how to present them. If you
have done anything more than the simplest experiment, you will find
that you have to choose between many possible ways of organizing and
presenting your results: for example, what summary statistics should
you include? Do you present a figure or a table? If you choose a figure,
should it be a histogram or a graph? If it is a graph, how will you
arrange the axes? And this is just the beginning! With experience, the
decisions will become much easier to make, but at first you will need to
spend some time thinking about presentation.

Organizing a Results section

There are two main aspects to a set of experimental data: the raw data
themselves and the results of any analysis of them that you choose to
do. A good *Results* section should contain both a summary of the data
and a report of the analyses. It is not unusual to see the *Results* section
of a psychology report begin along these lines: "An analysis of variance
was done on the data and there was a significant main effect for X."
This is not very informative. As a general rule, you should start with a
brief summary of your main findings, and then lead your reader
through the data, one level of analysis at a time, providing enough
information to justify the conclusions that you will draw in the *Discussion*. At this point you should make no interpretations of your data:
simply present all the important results, whether or not they are
favourable to your hypothesis. Deal with the main findings first,
before going on to the secondary results.

Summarize the main results with descriptive statistics

Obviously, for most of your experiments, you cannot simply report all your raw data. When you are measuring some characteristic of living organisms, there will almost always be variability across individuals or even within individuals over successive measurements. For this reason it is usual to make repeated measurements of the same thing and take an average. Typically, you would begin by reporting your group means, together with some measure of variability. For example, in an experiment that examined the effect of cartoon content on number of aggressive acts in children (assuming you had ethics approval for such a study), you might summarize your results this way:

> Children who watched violent cartoons engaged in a larger number of aggressive acts ($\underline{M}$ = 7.3, $\underline{SD}$ = 1.2) than those who watched non-violent cartoons ($\underline{M}$ = 4.1, $\underline{SD}$ = 1.9).

A brief summary like this is appropriate if you have only one or two variables to deal with. But what if your experiment has been more complex? Let's say that you were still asking questions about TV violence and aggression in children. In this case, though, you wanted to know whether cartoons have different effects from live-action violence, and if the effects are different for boys and girls. Now you have eight means to report rather than just two. At this point you might want to consider using a data table.

Data tables

If you can make your data summary clearer by using a table, by all means do so. However, it's essential that the tables themselves be well-organized and clear. Don't overload them with data, and be sure to plan the layout carefully. For the above example you might do something along the lines of Table 1 (see p. 54).

With a table like this, the reader can see the results at a glance. A good table should be self-explanatory. Nevertheless, it's important to refer to each table in the text and point out the most important aspects, without repeating everything it contains. For example:

> Table 1 shows that exposure to either cartoon or live-action TV violence increases the number of aggressive acts by children. This table also shows that girls exposed to live-action violence appear to become most aggressive.

Table 1

Number of violent acts by children following exposure to TV violence

	Cartoons				Live action			
	Violent		Non-violent		Violent		Non-violent	
Group	M	(SD)	M	(SD)	M	(SD)	M	(SD)
Boys	6.7[a]	(2.1)	4.3	(2.8)	6.4	(1.9)	4.7	(1.6)
Girls	5.4	(1.5)	3.8	(1.2)	7.1	(3.3)	4.0	(1.4)

Note. The means represent the number of observed aggressive actions during a half-hour observation period.
[a] One child in this group did not complete the whole experiment and was dropped from the analysis.

Preparing tables

The tables in this chapter were prepared according to APA guidelines. Among the most important points to remember are these:

1. Everything in the table should be double-spaced, including the titles and any notes at the bottom.

2. Each table should have a brief, informative heading.

3. Do not use any vertical lines anywhere in the table. If necessary, use extra spacing to make the table easier to read.

4. Make sure that each column has a heading.

5. Explain any abbreviations or special symbols you use in a note.

6. If you have made statistical comparisons between items in the table, be sure to identify them with asterisks and give the significance levels in a note.

7. If you do use notes to clarify information in the paper, they should be listed in this order: *general notes* that provide information relating to the table as a whole; *specific notes* that refer to individual cells in the table and are identified by superscript lower-case letters (for example, mentioning that a subject dropped out from a group); and *probability notes* that indicate the significance levels used.

These technical requirements aside, you should also ask yourself several questions:

• Do you have a brief, informative title on each table?
• Do the data in the table complement — rather than duplicate — what is in the text? You should avoid repetition as far as possible.

- Are the tables numbered sequentially throughout the paper?
- Is the style of the tables consistent throughout?
- Have you referred to the table in the text?

Tables or figures?

A table gives you one way to present your data, but you must always ask whether that is the most effective way of getting your point across. Tables have the advantage of being more exact, because they provide precise numerical data, but figures often give a more compelling impression of the overall pattern of results. Your decision to make a table rather than a figure should be based on which will convey the information most effectively. In general, a table is a good choice if the numbers you need to present might not be clear enough in the body of the text, but they don't make a point that would merit a figure.

Data figures

Sometimes the choice between a table and a figure comes down to personal style or preference. For example, let's reconsider the data in Table 1. You could present these data very easily in the form of a bar graph, as shown in Figure 1.

In this figure we have chosen to make two separate bar graphs, one for cartoons and one for live action. We have also chosen to juxtapose the violent/non-violent bars for the closest comparisons. If the emphasis of the study had been on sex differences in behaviour, we might have put the boy/girl columns next to each other. Depending on what aspects of your data you want to emphasize, you will have to decide which is the best way to arrange your figure.

In this last example, there is no strong reason for choosing either a figure or a table. However, if you have a lot of data and the point they make might be unclear even with a large table, then a figure is your best choice. Figures are also particularly useful when you are looking at functional relationships, where you change the value of an independent variable and look for changes in the dependent variable. As with tables, be sure to refer to each figure in the text and mention the major points that it illustrates.

Now let's suppose that, instead of showing all the children the same violence-containing scenes, you varied the number of violent acts in the films in order to see whether quantity has an effect. One way of reporting such data is in the form of a table, as shown in Table 2.

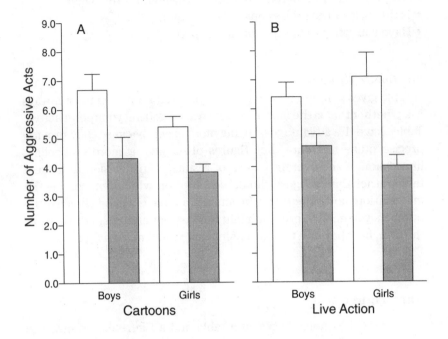

Figure 1. Mean number (+ SE) of aggressive acts by children following exposure to TV violence. Panel A: cartoon scenes; panel B: live action. Open bars: violent scenes; stippled bars: non-violent scenes. Error bars = 1 SEM.

These numbers suggest that there is a tendency for boys to show increasing aggression with increasing exposure up to a point, whereas girls show an increase followed by a decrease. A data table of this sort is an acceptable way of presenting your results, although if you tried to include a measure of variability, the table would start to become cluttered. Contrast this table with a figure showing the same set of data. In Figure 2 you can see at a glance how differently the two groups react.

Table 2

Number of aggressive acts by children following exposure to TV violence

	Number of violent incidents in TV film							
Group	0	1	2	3	4	5	6	7
Boys	.3	1.4	2.3	2.6	3.3	5.6	5.8	5.7
Girls	.2	1.1	2.5	3.8	4.1	3.2	2.4	1.2

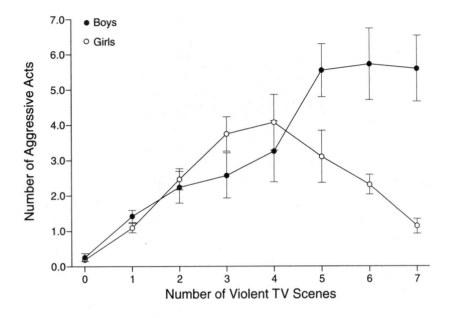

Figure 2. Mean number (+ /–SD) of aggressive acts for boys and girls as a function of the number of violent TV scenes to which they were exposed.

The actual numbers are probably less important than the *pattern* of results shown in the figure. In addition, a figure like this makes it easy to represent the variability in the data.

Figures need not be limited to simple line or bar graphs. Sometimes a pie chart will be more appropriate. Suppose that, to determine how students actually spent their time while they were "working," you had asked each of a group of students to keep track of the amount of time they spent in various activities. You could present your data in a table, simply listing the percentage of time spent doing different things; or you could draw a bar graph to make the point more graphically. In this case, however, you could probably make the greatest impression by presenting a pie chart, as in Figure 3. Here it is easy to see that your sample of students actually spent less than 60 per cent of their "work time" doing things that might be construed as work.

There are many ways to present your data graphically. Figures that are informative and well-presented can make the difference between a mediocre grade and a good one.

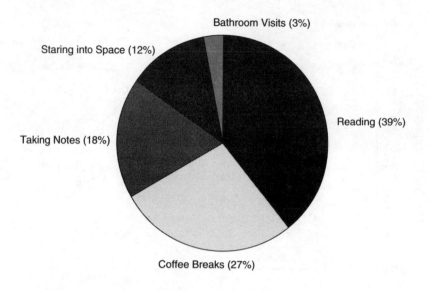

Figure 3. Percentage of time students spent in different activities during an evening session when they were "working."

Preparing figures

Most of the figures you present will take the form of graphs. Even without a software graphics package, the graphics capabilities of some word-processing systems can allow you to produce quite professional-looking figures. If you don't have access to a computer it's especially important to make your figures as neat as possible, but even if you do use one, there are some rules you should follow. In either case, the APA guidelines will be helpful:

1. Use a ruler and black ink for your drawing. If you are not working in a lab book, consider drawing a rough version on graph paper and then tracing it onto plain paper.

2. The independent variable (the one you have manipulated) should be on the horizontal axis, and the dependent variable (the one you measure) on the vertical axis.

3. The vertical axis should be about three-quarters the length of the horizontal one.

4. Use large and distinctive symbols, with different symbols for each line on the graph.

5. Label the axes clearly. Start each main word with a capital and run the axis label parallel to the axis. Always include the unit of measurement on the axis label.

6. Show only essential detail. A cluttered graph is difficult to read.

7. Include a legend describing the figure and indicating what the different symbols represent.

Of course there are many other refinements you could make. But even if you follow only the suggestions mentioned here, your figures will be much better than your instructor is accustomed to seeing in student lab reports.

Present the results of your statistical analyses

After you have described your data, the next step is to present the results of any statistical tests you have done. If the analysis is a straightforward one, you can report it directly in the text, giving enough information for the reader to confirm that the analysis has been done correctly. The exact information will vary with the test, but may include the value of the test statistic, the degrees of freedom, a measure of variability, and the level of statistical significance. If your analysis is a complicated one—for example, a multi-factor analysis of variance, or one involving a series of correlations—you might consider using a statistical table showing all the details of your analysis. As you become more experienced at presenting data, it will become easier to decide what to include in the text or in tables. Initially, though, you should refer to the *APA Manual*, or ask your instructor what is required.

In many experiments you are testing a hypothesis. Even if you are asking a question for which you do not have a specific prediction, you may set your experiment up formally as a test of a statistical hypothesis. For example, the question "What is the effect of different drugs on the rate of learning in rats?" could be rephrased as a statement: "Drug A produces significantly better learning than drug B." You could then test that hypothesis using the appropriate statistical tests.

You should present the actual statistical values and then a brief statement of what they mean. Although you may know exactly what your F-ratios imply, your reader may not. For example, in the drugs and learning experiment you might have analyzed your data using an analysis of variance. You could describe the results of this analysis by saying:

The analysis of variance showed a significant difference in the effectiveness of the two drugs $F(1, 15) = 14.5$, $p < .01$). The rats that were given drug A took fewer trials to learn the task than those that received drug B.

Above all, try to express your ideas as clearly as possible.

Finally, if you have performed several different analyses on your data, you should start by reporting the overall analysis and then move on to the secondary analyses. Remember, you are leading the reader through your paper, and the better your organization, the clearer it will be.

7

APA editorial style

The last three chapters have offered you guidelines on how to prepare a research paper and a lab report. Their main goal was to get you to think about how to organize your thoughts and your writing so that you can present your story clearly. Now it is time to consider the style of that presentation. In this context, the term "style" has two different meanings. The first refers to the manner in which we express our ideas: the words we choose, the length of sentences, and so on. This expressive style is discussed in Chapter 9. The second kind of style is editorial and concerns the physical arrangement of the words on the paper. For anyone working in psychology, the definitive style reference is the *Publication Manual of the American Psychological Association*, now in its fourth edition (American Psychological Association, 1994).

Although the *APA Manual* is directed mainly to those who publish in journals sponsored by the Association, its rules on format and style have been adopted by several disciplines as a guide for publishing as well as for student papers and theses. These guidelines can be applied to most scientific writing, even in disciplines that do not explicitly use APA style.

The main difference between a student paper and a manuscript submitted for publication is that the first is a final version, while the second, which may eventually be published, must follow different conventions in order to be prepared for typesetting; for example, text that is to be set in *italics* must be underlined in the submitted manuscript, and the text should be ragged—not justified—on the right. Check with your instructor to find out what you should do in a particular course. Here we will assume that what you are writing will not be submitted to a publisher, and hence should correspond as closely as possible to a published version.

Rules of presentation

The *APA manual* devotes 174 pages to APA editorial style, covering everything from the major organizational headings to when a comma should precede the word *and*. Here we will describe only the guidelines that are most important for undergraduate papers. For more details, refer to the manual itself.

Paper format

Use a single side of each page and double-space the entire paper, including the references. Every page, including the first, should be numbered, with arabic numerals, in the top-right hand corner. It's also good practice to use a *page header* — a short version of the title — at the top of each page, either immediately above or just to the left of the page number; that way, if any pages get separated they will be easy to identify. Always leave generous margins — at least 2.5 cm on all sides — so your instructor can add comments. In a submitted paper, tables and tables are always placed at the end of the manuscript, but for a student paper, it is usual to incorporate the tables and figures into the text. Normally you should place these on a separate sheet, immediately following the page where they are first referred to. Depending on the rules for your course, the figure legend may be placed either under the figure itself or on a separate page, facing the figure.

Headings and subheadings

When you are writing a library research paper it is sometimes useful to break down the paper into several sections; when you write a lab report it is essential. APA style permits up to five levels of headings and subheadings (if you can't produce italics, use underlining):

LEVEL FIVE
(centred, upper case)
Level One
(centred, upper- and lower-case)
Level Two
(centred, upper- and lower-case, italicized)

Level Three
(flush left, upper- and lower-case, italicized)
    Level four. (indented paragraph heading, italicized, lower-case after initial letter, ending with a period and leading directly into paragraph).

You will not often need to use all of these levels; in most cases, two will be adequate:

Method	(Level 1)
Apparatus and Procedure	(Level 3)

If you need a third level, add level 4:

Method	(Level 1)
Subjects	(Level 3)
Control group.	(Level 4)

If you had a series of experiments to describe, you might need to rearrange the headings:

Experiment 1	(Level 1)
Method	(Level 2)
Subjects	(Level 3)
Control group.	(Level 4)

The most important thing to remember is that headings should follow a logical and consistent pattern. Always start with Level 1 (except for a 5-level paper) and work down. You may not use every level in each section, but you should ensure that equivalent sections or sections of equal importance have the same level of heading.

Units of measurement

All APA journals require that any measurements be expressed in metric units, in most cases using the International System of Units (SI). You should report the metric equivalents even if you did not make your original measurements in those units. For clarity you may want to report both: e.g. "The platform was placed 15 in. (38.1 cm) above the landing surface." You should also be sure to use the appropriate SI abbreviations for the units.

Numbers. In general, you should use figures to express all numbers greater than nine (10 and above) and numbers below 10 that are used in comparisons with numbers above 10: for example, "5 out of 20 subjects reported that . . .". Other items that should be expressed in figures include all numbers relating to measurement, statistical and mathematical functions; times, dates and ages; numbers of subjects in an experiment; and numbers that describe part of a series. In most other circumstances—for example, when the number begins a sentence, or when expressing a fractional value—you should use words. When in doubt, go with the form that makes your statement easiest to read.

Quotations

We have already stressed the importance of acknowledging any quotations that you use. You should also be aware of how to present the quotations in the text.

Short quotations. If the quotation contains fewer than 40 words, enclose it in double quotation marks ("...") and include it as part of the text.

Long quotations. A longer quotation is set off from the main body of the text by indenting the whole quotation five to seven spaces from the left margin. Although APA style does not require it, you might ask your instructor whether you should also indent on the right. The quotation should not begin with a paragraph indent, but additional paragraphs should be indented from the new left margin. You do not need quotation marks for this kind of block quotation.

Quotes within quotes. If the passage you are quoting includes material already in quotation marks, make these single if the main quotation is in running text and double if it is set off as a block quotation.

Additions and omissions. If you change any words within the quotation—for instance, to maintain grammatical sense—the non-original words should be enclosed in [brackets], not (parentheses). When you omit part of a quotation, indicate the missing section with an ellipsis: three periods with a space before and after each one (...). If the omission is between sentences, include the original period (without a space) before the ellipsis.

Acknowledging sources. You should acknowledge the source of the quotation in the text, giving the page number(s) as well as the author and year. The complete reference should be contained in the reference list. The following chapter describes this format.

Reference
American Psychological Association (1994). *Publication manual of the American Psychological Association.* (4th ed.) Washington, DC: Author.

Chapter

8

Documentation in the sciences

In psychology there is a uniform style for referring to the sources you have consulted. However, the methods of documentation in the other sciences differ quite widely, even within a discipline. Always check with your instructor to make sure you are following the preferred practice for the course you are taking. Some instructors are very strict about citation practices; others will give you more freedom. The most important thing to remember is that your citations must be accurate.

Documentation in scientific writing differs from that in the humanities in two important ways:

1. Instead of footnotes, there are brief references (citations) in the text itself.

2. Instead of a bibliography, there is a *Reference* section at the end of the paper, which lists only those works referred to directly in the text; other works are not listed.

There are two main styles of citation in scientific writing: alphabetic and consecutive. But within each style you have several ways of citing the references in the text. The format for listing the work in the *References* section also varies widely. This chapter will show you the most common citation formats and suggest journals that you may use as models. Although this chapter will concentrate on APA reference style because it is used so widely, it will also mention some alternatives.

Alphabetical citation — APA reference style

The most widely used alphabetical system is the one defined in the *APA Manual*. Virtually all psychological publications, as well as many in the social sciences and other disciplines, use this format.

Citation in the text

The author-date format is used for all citations. In this format the author's surname and the year of publication are inserted into the text at the appropriate points:

> Birchmore (1993) studied the children of alcoholics . . .
> In a study of children of alcoholics (Birchmore, 1993) . . .
> In 1993, Birchmore reported . . .

If there are two authors, include both names every time you cite the reference in the text. Use an ampersand (&) when the names are in parentheses, but "and" in the running text:

> Leventhal and Lipsitt (1964) reported that neonates did not differentiate between small frequency differences, but others have found that they will orient better to high than to low frequency sounds (Morrongiello & Clifton, 1984).

If there are between two and six authors, cite all the names when the reference first occurs, and afterwards cite only the first author, followed by "et al." For six or more authors, the text citation should contain only the name of the first author, followed by "et al.":

> Pola, Wyatt and Lustgarten (1992) studied eye movements . . .

then:

> Pola et al. (1992) found that subjects suppressed movements . . .

Note that the year should be included the first time a work is cited in a paragraph, but not in subsequent citations within that paragraph (unless you mention more than one work by the same author).

Organization of citations within parentheses. If you cite more than one item in a single set of parentheses, arrange them as follows:

1. Several papers by a single author ordered chronologically:

> (Smith, 1969, 1973, 1980, in press)

2. Several papers by the same author in the same year ordered with suffixes a, b, c, etc., after the year:

> (Smith, 1992a, 1992b)

3. Several papers by different authors in alphabetical order according to authors' surnames:

> (Aardvark, 1994; Smith, 1992a, 1992b; Zebra, 1932)

Referring to a specific part of a source. When referring to a particular part of a source, give the specific location. Always give the page number if you quote a source:

(Cormack, Stevenson, & Schor, 1994, pp. 2601-2602)

(Schmidt, 1994, Figure 2)

Citing a source in parenthetical material. If you enclose a statement in parentheses, don't use additional parentheses to cite the source:

(refer to Hubel & Wiesel, 1962, for more technical details)

Citing a work that you have not read yourself. Sometimes, if you are unable to locate an original work, you may have to rely on a description in a secondary source. In this case you should cite the secondary source that you have read and include only that work in the *References*:

The results of Wilcox and Wolf (as cited in Symons & Pearson, 1994) . . .

Numerical citations

An alternative to the author-date citation required by APA style is the numerical citation. Several biological and medical journals use this style, in which the source is cited as a number that corresponds to the reference listed in the *References* section. The cited references are set either in parentheses or as superscripts in the appropriate places.

Several authors have described this phenomenon.[18,23,31]

Several authors have described this phenomenon.[18]

Some journals (such as *Nature* and *Science*) list the references in the *References* section in the order of their first citation in the paper. Others use numeric citations in the text but arrange the reference list in alphabetical order. In this case the citation numbers in the text cannot be assigned until all the references have been collated: if you take out or add any references, you will need to change the citation numbers.

Citation in the *References* section

The reference list is an extremely important part of your paper. It should contain every work that you have cited in the text — and none that you have not cited. (To include uncited references is fabrication.)

The precise format of the reference list varies between disciplines and journals. Here again we concentrate on the APA reference format, but most of the general rules about the organization of the reference list are similar across disciplines. The differences occur primarily in the placement of publication date, authors' initials, use of abbreviations, and punctuation. If your discipline does not use APA style explicitly, ask your instructor which journal to use as a model.

In an APA-formatted manuscript the first letter of the reference has a normal paragraph indent. The published format sets the first letter flush with the left margin and indents subsequent lines three spaces. You should capitalize only the first word of the title and the subtitle, if there is one. The date of publication follows immediately after the authors' names. The titles of books and journals are underlined in manuscript format (italicized in published form), as are the volume numbers of the journals.

The most important APA requirements (with comments on non-APA variations) are these:

1. Arrange the references alphabetically.
2. When citing more than one work by the same author or authors, list them chronologically. For works published in the same year, add the letter suffix (1982a, etc.), as you did in the text.
3. Begin with the first author's surname, followed by the initials.
4. If there is more than one author, list all the names. (In some biological journals, only the first three authors are listed. Depending on the discipline, subsequent authors' initials either precede or follow their surnames).
5. Give the full title of the article, chapter, or book.
6. When you are referring to journals, write out the title in full. (If your discipline's style permits abbreviations, use the standard forms).
7. Always give the year, volume, and page numbers.

Sample entries

The following examples cover the most common sources. To cite different kinds of work, check the detailed instructions in the *APA Manual*. For examples, you can also look in the *References* section of any journal published by the American Psychological Association.

Journals:

King, F.L., & Kimura, D. (1972). Left-ear superiority in dichotic perception of vocal nonverbal sounds. Canadian Journal of Psychology, 26, 111-116.

Broerse, J., & Grimbeck, P. (1994). Eye movements and the associative basis of contingent color after-effects: A comment on Siegel, Allan, and Eissenberg (1992). Journal of Experimental Psychology: General, 123, 81-85.

Magazine articles:

If you are referring to an article in a magazine, you should also include both the volume number and the date shown on the issue—month and date for weeklies such as *Science* and *Nature*, month only for monthlies:

Horgan, J. (1994, July). Can science explain consciousness? Scientific American, 271, 88-94.

Books:

For books published in the United States give the city and state of publication as well as the publisher; for the state, use the US Postal Service's two-letter abbreviations. For books published elsewhere give the province or country of publication. There are a few exceptions to these rules. Major cities that are well-known publishing centres, such as Toronto, San Francisco, Amsterdam, or London, do not require further identification.

Locke, J.L. (1993). The child's path to spoken language. Cambridge, MA: Harvard University Press.

If the reference is a second or subsequent edition, be sure to include that information immediately following the title.

Gleitman, H. (1995). Psychology (4th ed.). New York: Norton.

Chapters in edited books:

In the text you should cite the authors of the chapter you have read, and then give both the chapter title and the full book reference in the *References* list. Although you don't need to give the number of the chapter, you should include the volume number for any multi-volume work. Note that the abbreviation for an edition of a book is "ed." and for an editor it is "Ed."

Nelson, C.A., & Horowitz, F.D. (1987). Visual motion perception in infancy: A review and synthesis. In P. Salapatek & L. Cohen (Eds.), Handbook of infant perception: Vol. 2. From perception to cognition. Orlando, FL: Academic Press.

These examples should cover most of the material that you are likely to cite in an undergraduate paper. For other examples you can look at the references in several of the chapters in this book. If you encounter a less common kind of reference, such as an abstract from a secondary source, a newspaper article, or a movie, consult the *APA Manual*.

Biology and the biomedical sciences

There is not a single standard format for the references in biological journals, although you can find some general rules in the *CBE Style Manual* (1983). Typically, journal titles are abbreviated; for the accepted forms, see the 1976 *Biosis List of Serials*. Placement of the year of publication, treatment of page numbers, and details of punctuation vary across journals in different disciplines. The *Canadian Journal of Zoology* is used as a model here, but you should check with your instructor for the requirements in your course.

Journals:

BURTON, M.P., and D.R. IDLER. 1984. The reproductive cycle of the winter flounder, Pseudopleuronectes americanus (Walbaum). Can. J. Zool. 62: 2563-2567.

Books:

WHYTE, M.A. 1975. Time, tide and the cockle. In Growth rhythms and the history of the earth's rotation. Edited by G.D. Rosenberg and S.K. Runcorn. John Wiley and Sons, London. pp.177-189.

References

American Psychological Association (1994). *Publication manual of the American Psychological Association.* (4th ed.). Washington, DC: Author.

Council of Biology Editors (1983). *CBE style manual: A guide for authors, editors, and publishers in the biological sciences.* (5th ed.). Bethesda, MD.: Author.

9

Writing with style

Writing style is no less important in the sciences than it is in any other discipline. It's true that scientific writing does not tend to go in for fancy words and extravagant images: after all, its main goal is to communicate clearly. But any style, from the simplest to the most elaborate, can be effective, depending on the occasion and intent. Writers known for their style are those who have projected something of their own personality into their writing; we can hear a distinctive voice in what they say. In any discipline, the most effective style is one that is clear, concise, and forceful.

Be clear

Choose clear words

A good dictionary is a wise investment; get into the habit of using one. It will give you not only common meanings, but less familiar applications and derivations, as well as proper spelling. Canadian usage and spelling may follow either British or American practices, but usually combine aspects of both; check before you buy a dictionary to be sure that it gives these variants.

A thesaurus lists words that are closely related in meaning. It can help when you want to avoid repeating yourself, or when you are fumbling for a word that's on the tip of your tongue. But be careful: make sure you remember the difference between denotative and connotative meanings. A word's denotation is its primary or "dictionary" meaning. Its connotations are any associations that it may suggest; they may not be as exact as the denotations, but they are part of the impression the word conveys. If you examine a list of "synonyms" in a thesaurus, you will see that even words with similar meanings can have dramatically different connotations. For example, alongside the word *indifferent* your thesaurus may give the following: *neutral, unconcerned, careless, easy-going, unambitious,* and *half-hearted.* Imagine the different impressions you would create if you chose one or the other of those words to complete this sentence: "Questioned about the project's chance of success, he was _____ in his response." In order to write clearly, you must remember that a reader may react to the suggestive meaning of a word as much as to its "dictionary" meaning.

Avoid jargon and use plain English

All academic subjects have their own specialized terminology; it may be unfamiliar to outsiders, but it helps specialists to explain things to each other. The trouble is that people sometimes use jargon—special, technical language—unnecessarily, thinking it will make them seem more knowledgeable. Too often the result is not clarity but confusion. The guideline is easy: use specialized terminology only when it's a kind of shorthand that will help you explain something more precisely and efficiently. If plain prose will do just as well, stick to it.

Plain words are almost always more forceful than fancy ones. If you aren't sure what plain English is, think of everyday speech: how do you talk to your friends? Many of our most common words—the ones that sound most natural and direct—are short. A good number of them are also among the oldest words in the English language. By contrast, most of the words that English has derived from other languages are longer and more complicated; even after they've been used for centuries, they can still sound artificial. For this reason you should beware of words loaded with prefixes (*pre-, post-, anti-, pro-, sub-, maxi-,* etc.) and suffixes (*-ate, -ize, -tion,* etc.). These Latinate attachments can make individual words more precise and efficient, but putting a lot of them together will make your writing seem dense and hard to understand. In many cases you can substitute a plain word for a fancy one:

Fancy	*Plain*
determinant	cause
utilization	use
cognizant	aware
obviate	prevent
terminate	end
infuriate	anger
conclusion	end

requisite	needed
numerous	many
finalize	finish, complete
systematize	order
sanitize	clean
remuneration	pay
maximization	increase

Suggesting that you write in plain English does not mean that you should never pick an unfamiliar, long, or foreign word: sometimes those words are the only ones that will convey precisely what you mean. Inserting an unusual expression into a passage of plain writing can also be an effective means of catching the reader's attention—as long as you don't do it too often.

Be precise

Always be as precise or exact as you can. Avoid all-purpose adjectives like *major, significant,* and *important,* and vague verbs such as *involved, entail,* and *exist,* when you can be more specific:

orig Catalysts <u>are involved</u> in many biochemical reactions.

rev. Catalysts <u>speed up</u> many biochemical reactions.

Here's another example:

orig. The discovery of genetic engineering techniques was a <u>significant</u> contribution to biological science.

rev. The discovery of genetic engineering techniques was a <u>dangerous</u> contribution to biological science.

(or)

rev. The discovery of genetic engineering techniques was a <u>beneficial</u> contribution to biological science.

Avoid unnecessary qualifiers
Qualifiers such as *very, rather,* and *extremely* are over-used. Saying that something is *very elegant* may have less impact than saying simply that it is *elegant.* For example, compare these sentences:

They devised an elegant hypothesis to explain their data.

They devised a very elegant hypothesis to explain their data.

Which has more punch?

When you think that an adjective needs qualifying—and sometimes it will—first see if it's possible to change either the adjective or the phrasing. Instead of writing:

Multinational Drugs made a very big profit last year.

write:

Multinational Drugs made an unprecedented profit last year.

or (if you aren't sure whether or not the profit actually set a record):

Multinational Drugs' profit rose forty per cent last year.

In some cases qualifiers not only weaken your writing but are redundant, since the adjectives themselves are absolutes. To say that something is *very unique* makes as much—or as little—sense as to say that someone is *slightly pregnant* or *very dead*.

Creating clear paragraphs

Paragraphs come in so many sizes and patterns that no single formula could possibly cover them all. The two basic principles to remember are these: (1) a paragraph is a means of developing and framing an idea or impression, and (2) the divisions between paragraphs aren't random, but indicate a shift in focus.

Develop your ideas

You are not likely to sit down and consciously ask yourself "What pattern shall I use to develop this paragraph?" What comes first is the idea you intend to develop: the pattern the paragraph takes should flow from the idea itself and the way you want to discuss or expand it.

You may take one or several paragraphs to develop an idea fully. For a definition alone you could write one paragraph or ten, depending on the complexity of the subject and the nature of the assignment. Just remember that ideas need development, and that each new paragraph signals a change in idea.

Consider the topic sentence

Skilled skim-readers know that they can get the general drift of a book simply by reading the first sentence of each paragraph. The reason is that most paragraphs begin by stating the central idea to be developed. If you are writing your essay from a formal plan, you will probably find that each section and subsection will generate the topic sentence for a new paragraph.

Like the thesis statement for the paper as a whole, the topic sentence is not obligatory: in some paragraphs the controlling idea is not stated until the middle or even the end, and in others it is not stated at all but merely implied. Nevertheless, it's a good idea to think out a topic sentence for every paragraph. That way you'll be sure that each one has a readily graspable point and is clearly connected to what comes before and after. When revising your initial draft, check to see that each paragraph is held together by a topic sentence, either stated or implied. If you find that you can't formulate one, you should probably rework the whole paragraph.

Maintain focus

To be clear a paragraph should contain only those details that are in some way related to the central idea. It must also be structured so that the details are easily seen to be related. One way of showing these relations is to keep the same grammatical subject in most of the sentences that make up the paragraph. When the grammatical subject is shifting all the time, a paragraph loses focus, as in the following example (Cluett & Ahlborn, 1965):

> Boys in school play a variety of sports these days. In the fall, football still attracts the most, although an increasing number now play soccer. For some, basketball is the favourite when the ball season is over, but you will find that swimming or gymnastics are also popular. Cold winter temperatures may allow the school to have an outdoor rink, and then hockey becomes a source of enjoyment for many. In spring, though, the rinks begin melting, and so there is less opportunity to play. Then some boys take up soccer again, while track and field also attracts many participants.

Here the grammatical subject (underlined) is constantly jumping from one thing to another. Notice how much stronger the focus becomes when all the sentences have the same grammatical subject — either the same noun, a synonym, or a related pronoun:

> Boys in school play a variety of sports these days. In the fall, most still choose football, although an increasing number now play soccer. When the ball season is over, some turn to basketball; others prefer swimming or gymnastics. If cold winter temperatures permit an outdoor rink, many boys enjoy hockey. Once the ice begins to melt in spring, though, they can play less often. Then some take up soccer again, while others choose track and field.

Naturally it's not always possible to retain the same grammatical subject throughout a paragraph. If you were comparing the athletic pursuits of boys and girls, for example, you would have to switch back and forth between boys and girls as your grammatical subject. In the same way, you will have to shift when you are discussing examples of an idea or exceptions to it.

Avoid monotony

If most or all of the sentences in your paragraph have the same grammatical subject, how do you avoid boring your reader? There are two easy ways:

Use stand-in words. Pronouns, either personal (*I*, *we*, *you*, *he*, *she*, *it*, *they*) or demonstrative (*this*, *that*, *those*) can stand in for the subject, as can synonyms (words or phrases that mean the same thing). The revised paragraph on boys' sports, for example, uses the pronouns *some*, *most*, and *they* as substitutes for *boys*. Most well-written paragraphs have a liberal sprinkling of these stand-in words.

"Bury" the subject by putting something in front of it. When the subject is placed in the middle of the sentence rather than at the beginning, it's less obvious to the reader. If you take another look at the revised paragraph, you'll see that in several sentences there is a word or phrase in front of the subject. Even a single word, such as *first*, *then*, *lately*, or *moreover*, will do the trick. (Incidentally, this is a useful technique to remember when you are writing a letter of application and want to avoid starting every sentence with *I*.)

Link your ideas

To create coherent paragraphs, you need to link your ideas clearly. Linking words are those connectors—conjunctions and conjunctive adverbs—that show the relations between one sentence, or part of a sentence, and another; they're also known as transition words, because they bridge the transition from one thought to another. Make a habit of using linking words when you shift from one grammatical subject or idea to another, whether the shift occurs within a single paragraph or as you move from one paragraph to the next. Here are some of the most common connectors and the logical relations they indicate:

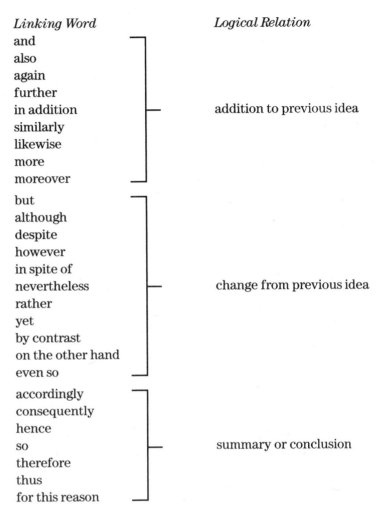

Linking Word	Logical Relation
and also again further in addition similarly likewise more moreover	addition to previous idea
but although despite however in spite of nevertheless rather yet by contrast on the other hand even so	change from previous idea
accordingly consequently hence so therefore thus for this reason	summary or conclusion

Numerical terms such as *first*, *second*, and *third* also work well as links.

Vary the length, but avoid extremes

Ideally, academic writing will have a comfortable balance of long and short paragraphs. Avoid the extremes, especially the one-sentence paragraph, which can only state an idea, without explaining or developing it. A series of very short paragraphs is usually a sign that you have not developed your ideas in enough detail, or that you have started new paragraphs unnecessarily. On the other hand, a succession of long paragraphs can be tiring and difficult to read. In deciding when to start a new paragraph, remember always to consider what is clearest and most helpful for the reader.

Be concise

At one time or another, you will probably be tempted to pad your writing. Whatever the reason—because you need to write two or three thousand words and have only enough to say for one thousand, or just because you think length is strength and hope to get a better mark for the extra—padding is a mistake. You may fool some of the people some of the time, but not often.

Strong writing is always concise. It leaves out anything that does not serve some communicative or stylistic purpose, in order to say as much as possible in as few words as possible. Concise writing will help you do better on both your essays and your exams.

Guidelines for concise writing

Use adverbs and adjectives sparingly
Avoid the shotgun approach to adverbs and adjectives; don't just spray your work with modifiers in the hope that one will hit. One well-chosen word is always better than a series of synonyms:

orig. As well as being costly and financially extravagant, the project is reckless and foolhardy.

rev. The venture is foolhardy as well as costly.

Avoid noun clusters
A recent trend in some writing is to use nouns as adjectives, as in the phrase *noun cluster*. This device can be effective occasionally, but frequent use can produce a monstrous pile-up of words. Breaking up noun clusters may not always produce fewer words, but it will make your writing easier to read:

orig. word-processor utilization manual

rev. manual for using word-processors

orig. pollution investigation committee

rev. committee to investigate pollution

Avoid chains of relative clauses
Sentences full of clauses beginning with *which, that,* or *who* are usually more wordy than necessary. Try reducing some of those clauses to phrases or single words:

orig. The solutions <u>which</u> were discussed last night have a practical benefit <u>which</u> is easily grasped by people <u>who</u> have no technical training.

rev. The solutions discussed last night have a practical benefit, easily grasped by non-technical people.

Try reducing clauses to phrases or words

Independent clauses can often be reduced by subordination. Here are a few examples:

orig. The report was written in a clear and concise manner and it was widely read.

better Written in a clear and concise manner, the report was widely read.

best Clear and concise, the report was widely read.

orig. His plan was of a radical nature and was a source of embarrassment to his employer.

rev. His radical plan embarrassed his employer.

For more detail on subordination and reduction, see p. 82.

Strike out hackneyed expressions and circumlocutions

Trite or roundabout phrases may flow from your pen or keyboard without a thought, but they make for stale prose. Unnecessary words are deadwood; be prepared to hunt and chop ruthlessly to keep your writing vital:

Wordy	*Revised*
due to the fact that	because
at this point in time	now
consensus of opinion	consensus
in the near future	soon
when all is said and done	(omit)
in the eventuality that	if
in all likelihood	likely

Avoid ''it is'' and ''there is'' beginnings

Although it may not always be possible, try to avoid *it is* or *there is* (*are*) beginnings. Your sentences will be crisper and more concise:

orig. There are only a few days in the year when the phenomenon may be observed.

rev. The phenomenon may be observed on only a few days of the year.

orig. It is certain that pollution will increase.

rev. Pollution will certainly increase.

Be forceful

Developing a forceful, vigorous style simply means learning some common tricks of the trade and practising them until they become habit.

Choose active over passive verbs

Scientists who publish in professional journals are divided on whether you should use the active or passive voice. Traditionally, most have preferred the passive voice ("The rat was placed in the starting box of the maze," rather than "I placed the rat in the starting box") because they believed that its impersonal quality helped to maintain the detached, impartial tone appropriate for a scientific report. Now the active voice is recommended because it is clearer and less likely to lead to awkward sentences. Remember, too, that you should use "I" rather than "we" if you were the only one doing the experiment.

An active verb creates more energy than a passive one does:

Active: She wiped up the spill.

Passive: The spill was wiped up by her.

Moreover, passive constructions tend to produce awkward, convoluted phrasing. Writers of bureaucratic documents are among the worst offenders:

> It has been decided that the utilization of small rivers in the province for purposes of generating hydro-electric power should be studied by our department and that a report to the Deputy should be made by our Director as soon as possible.

The passive verbs in this mouthful make it hard to tell who is doing what.

Passive verbs are appropriate in two specific cases:

1. When the situation described is in fact passive—that is, when the subject of the sentence is the passive recipient of some action.

2. When using a passive verb will help to maintain focus by eliminating the need to shift to a different subject. The following example has both reasons for using the passive verb *were eaten*:

The guppies had adjusted to their new tank but <u>were eaten</u> by the larger fish a short time later.

Use personal subjects

Most of us find it more interesting to learn about people than about things—hence the enduring appeal of the gossip columns. Wherever possible, therefore, make the subjects of your sentences personal. This trick goes hand-in-hand with use of active verbs. Almost any sentence becomes more lively with active verbs and a personal subject:

orig. The materialistic implications of <u>Darwin's theory</u> led to a long delay before it <u>was published</u>.

rev. <u>Darwin delayed</u> publication of <u>his theory</u> for a long time because of its materialistic implications.

Here's another example:

orig. It <u>may be concluded</u> that the reaction <u>had been permitted</u> to continue until it was completed because <u>there was no sign</u> of any precipitate when the flask <u>was examined</u>.

rev. <u>We may conclude</u> that the reaction <u>had finished</u> because <u>we could not see</u> any precipitate when <u>we examined</u> the flask.

Use concrete details

Concrete details are easier to understand—and to remember—than abstract theories. Whenever you are discussing abstract concepts, therefore, always provide specific examples and illustrations; if you have a choice between a concrete word and an abstract one, choose the concrete. Consider this sentence:

Watson and Crick were the first to demonstrate the geometrical structure of DNA.

Now see how a few specific details can bring the facts to life:

Watson and Crick showed that the DNA molecule was arranged as a double helix and that this organization helped explain how genetic material could be replicated.

Suggesting that you add concrete details doesn't mean getting rid of all abstractions. It's simply a plea to balance them with accurate details. This is one occasion when added wording, if it is concrete and correct, can improve your writing.

Make important ideas stand out

Experienced writers know how to manipulate sentences in order to emphasize certain points. Here are some of their techniques:

Place key words in strategic positions

The positions of emphasis in a sentence are the beginning and, above all, the end. If you want to bring your point home with force, don't put the key words in the middle of the sentence. Save them for the last:

> *orig* · People are less afraid of losing wealth than of losing face in this image-conscious society.

> *new* · In this image-conscious society people are less afraid of losing wealth than of losing face.

Subordinate minor ideas

Small children connect incidents with a string of "ands," as if everything were of equal importance:

> We went to the zoo and we saw a lion and John spilled his drink.

As they grow up, however, they learn to subordinate: that is, to make one part of a sentence less important in order to emphasize another point:

> Because the bus was delayed, we missed our class.

Major ideas stand out more and connections become clearer when minor ideas are subordinated:

> Spring arrived and we had nothing to do.

> When spring arrived, we had nothing to do.

Make your most important idea the subject of the main clause, and try to put it at the end, where it will be most emphatic:

> I was relieved when I saw my marks.

> When I saw my marks, I was relieved.

Vary sentence structure

As with anything else, variety adds spice to writing. One way of adding variety, which will also make an important idea stand out, is to use a periodic rather than a simple sentence structure.

Most sentences follow the simple pattern of subject — verb — object (plus modifiers):

> The dog bit the man on the ankle.
>   s   v   o

A simple sentence such as this gives the main idea at the beginning and therefore creates little tension. A *periodic sentence*, on the other hand, does not give the main clause until the end, following one or more subordinate clauses:

> Because there was little demand for his course, in the following year it was cancelled.
> $\underline{\text{s}}$ $\underline{\text{v}}$

The longer the periodic sentence is, the greater the suspense and the more emphatic the final part. Since this high-tension structure is more difficult to read than the simple sentence, your readers would be exhausted if you used it too often. Save it for those times when you want to make a point with particular force.

Vary sentence length

A short sentence can add punch to an important point, especially when it comes as a surprise. This technique can be particularly useful for conclusions. Don't overdo it, though. A string of long sentences may be monotonous, but a string of short ones has a staccato effect that can make your writing sound like a child's reader: "This is my dog. See him run."

Use contrast

Just as a jeweller will highlight a diamond by displaying it against dark velvet, so you can highlight an idea by placing it against a contrasting background:

> *orig* · Most employees in industry do not have indexed pensions.

> *rev.* Unlike civil servants, most employees in industry do not have indexed pensions.

Using parallel phrasing will increase the effect of the contrast:

> Although he often gave informal talks, he seldom gave presentations at conferences.

Use a well-placed adverb or correlative construction

Adding an adverb or two can sometimes help you to dramatize a concept:

> *orig* · Although I dislike the proposal, I must accept it as the practical answer.

> *rev.* Although <u>emotionally</u> I dislike the concept, <u>intellectually</u> I must accept it as the practical answer.

Correlatives such as *both . . . and* or *not only . . . but also* can be used to emphasize combinations as well:

orig · Smith was a good teacher and a good friend.

rev. Smith was <u>both</u> a good teacher <u>and</u> a good friend.

rev. Smith was <u>not only</u> a good teacher <u>but also</u> a good friend.

Use your ears

Your ears are probably your best critics: make good use of them. Before producing a final copy of any piece of writing, read it out loud, in a clear voice. The difference between cumbersome and fluent passages will be unmistakable.

A note on the use of neutral language

The guiding principles of the fourth edition of the *APA Manual* are "specificity" and "sensitivity." "Specificity" in this context refers to the fact that researchers need to provide enough specific information about their study for someone else to replicate it. "Sensitivity" means that the language used in writing a paper should not contain evaluative terms that might be considered pejorative. The authors suggest, for example, that "Oriental" be replaced with "Asian," or a reference to the precise country of origin. They make a number of suggestions for unbiased language when referring to gender, race, sexual orientation, and disability. In brief, the language that you use in a paper should not demean people, either by denying their individuality or by referring to them inaccurately. For example, the APA guidelines would suggest using "blind individuals" or "people with disabilities" rather than a group designation such as "the blind" or "the disabled."

The question of what constitutes biased writing is a difficult one because there are so many different points of view. No matter how hard you try, it's unlikely that you will be able to satisfy everyone. The most successful strategy when you are writing is to make sure that you do not take traditional assumptions for granted. For example, it is no longer accurate to assume that doctors or researchers are all male, or that nurses and research assistants are necessarily female. Wherever possible you should use specific, or neutral, or inclusive terms, and you should always be alert to the possibility that you are misrepresenting a group. However, in our view you should not tie your writing in knots to satisfy all demands for neutrality and correctness. You should also be aware that what is acceptable may change over time, so that a word that is correct today may not be correct five years from now.

Some final advice: write before you revise

No one would expect you to sit down and put all this advice into practice as soon as you start to write. You would feel so constrained that it would be hard to get anything down on paper at all. You will be better off if you begin practising these techniques during the editing process, when you are looking critically at what you have already written. Some experienced writers can combine the creative and critical functions, but most of us find it easier to write a rough draft first, before starting the detailed task of revising.

Reference

Cluett, R., & Ahlborn, L. (1965). *Effective English prose.* New York: L.W. Singer.

10

Writing examinations

If you are like most students, you will face many exams over the course of your university career. They come in all shapes and sizes, ranging from essay exams to the multiple-choice type, as well as those requiring true-false answers, filling in diagrams, or solving problems. This chapter offers some suggestions that should help you to cope with exams.

General guidelines

Before the exam

No matter what type of examination you take, you need to be prepared. This does not mean sitting down a couple of nights beforehand and trying to read and remember everything in your textbook. It does not even mean reading passively through your notes and texts once a week throughout the term. Studying is an active process, and if you develop good study skills you will be well on your way to success in whatever exams you may take.

The strategy suggested here is the one developed by the study-skills counsellors at the University of Western Ontario. You can adapt it to fit your own needs. The most important thing to remember is to be organized and to use your time effectively. For more information on study skills and examination-writing see Fleet, Goodchild, and Zajchowski (1994).

There are six steps to consider in preparing for an exam:

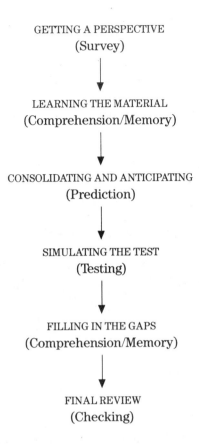

GETTING A PERSPECTIVE
(Survey)

LEARNING THE MATERIAL
(Comprehension/Memory)

CONSOLIDATING AND ANTICIPATING
(Prediction)

SIMULATING THE TEST
(Testing)

FILLING IN THE GAPS
(Comprehension/Memory)

FINAL REVIEW
(Checking)

1. Getting a perspective

Exam preparation has to begin long before the exam period itself. In fact, you should start organizing and collating your materials as soon as you have the course outline and know what kind of exams you will be taking. Then, as you progress through the term, you should be reading and taking notes in a form that will be useful when the exam finally comes around.

As the exam period approaches, gather together all the materials you have accumulated during the course—textbook, course outline, lecture notes, notes you have made yourself from the textbook, and so on. Skim through this material to remind yourself of the main topic areas. Even at this stage, you should be able to identify general areas from which questions might be drawn.

2. Learning the material

You can make this stage much easier if you have spent some time after each lecture reviewing both your notes and the text. Weekly review will help you not only to remember important material but to relate new information to old. If you don't review regularly, at the end of the year you'll be faced with relearning rather than remembering.

Set memory triggers. As you review, condense and focus the material by writing down in the margin key words or phrases that will trigger off a whole set of details in your mind. The trigger might be a concept word that names or points to an important theory or definition, or a quantitative phrase such as "three factors affecting the development of schizophrenia" or "four classes of operant conditioning."

Sometimes you can create an acronym or a nonsense sentence that will trigger an otherwise hard-to-remember set of facts—something like the mnemonic "Oh, Oh, Oh, To Touch And Feel A Green Ververt At Home" for the initial letters of the twelve cranial nerves. Because the difficulty of memorizing increases with the number of individual items you are trying to remember, any method that will reduce the number will increase your effectiveness.

At this stage you can benefit from rewriting your notes and condensing them so that you can go through them quickly during your final review. This is also the time to make sure you understand all the material. Trying to learn by rote something you don't understand is far more difficult than simply hanging facts on a well-understood framework.

Whatever your study plan, don't just read through your text and other course materials without making notes, asking questions, or solving problems. Something that seems quite straightforward when you read it may turn out to be much less clear when you have to write about it.

3. Consolidating and anticipating

Here you should be thinking specifically about what questions may be on the exam. The best way to do this is to analyze the course material, both main ideas and details, and then try to make up questions based on it. Rephrasing the material in the form of questions that might be asked should make it easier to recognize and remember when you are in the exam room.

In addition, you should try to look over some previous question papers. Old examinations are useful both for seeing the types of question you might be asked and for checking on the thoroughness of your preparation. If old exams aren't available, you might get together with friends who are taking the same course and ask each other questions. Just remember that the most useful review questions are not the ones that require you to recall facts, but those that force you to analyze, integrate, or evaluate information.

4. Simulating the test

Set a hypothetical exam for yourself, based on old exam questions and/ or ones that you have made up. Then find a time when you will be free of interruptions and write the exam as if it were the real thing. Although this takes a lot of self-discipline, it's an excellent way to find out your strengths and weaknesses.

5. Filling in the gaps

By now you should have a good idea of which areas need further study. Go over them carefully. Don't waste time on things that you know well: just fill in the gaps.

6. Final review

The day before the exam, go over your condensed notes and rehearse some possible questions. At this stage you should have done all of the basic work of making sure you understand and remember the material. What you need now is to get yourself into the best possible frame of mind.

Test anxiety

Most students feel nervous before examinations. It's not surprising. Writing an exam of any kind imposes strong pressures. In an essay exam, because the time is restricted, you can't edit and rewrite the way you can in a regular essay; and because the questions are restricted, you must write on topics you might otherwise choose to avoid. If you are writing a multiple-choice exam, often you don't know whether you are interpreting the questions correctly. Also, if there is a penalty for guessing you have the stress of deciding whether to mark an answer that you aren't sure is correct. You know that to do your best you need to feel calm—but how? It may be of some small comfort to know that a moderate level of anxiety is beneficial: it keeps you alert. It's when you are overconfident or paralyzed with fear that you run into difficulties.

There are many strategies for coping with test anxiety, but perhaps the best general advice is to try to control your stress in a positive way. For example, give yourself lots of time to get to the exam; don't worry about how other students might be performing; don't keep generating negative "what if" possibilities. Even if you can't turn off your worries, you can reduce them to a point where you will be able to perform well.

At the exam

If you look at the question paper and your first reaction is "I can't do any of it!", force yourself to keep calm; take ten slow, deep breaths as a deliberate relaxation exercise. Decide which is the question that you can answer best. Even if the exam seems impossible at first, you can probably find one question that looks manageable: that's the one to begin with. It will get you rolling and increase your confidence. By the time you have finished, you are likely to find that your mind has worked through to the answer for another question.

Essay examinations

Read the exam
An exam is not a hundred-metre dash; instead of starting to write immediately, take time at the beginning to read through each question and create a plan of action. A few minutes spent on thinking and organizing will bring better results than the same time spent on writing a few more lines.

Apportion your time
Read the instructions carefully to find out how many questions you must answer and to see if you have any choice. Subtract five minutes or so for the initial planning, then divide the time you have left by the number of questions you have to answer. If possible, allow for a little extra time at the end to reread and edit your work. If the instructions on the exam indicate that not all questions are of equal value, apportion your time accordingly.

Choose your questions
Decide on the questions that you will do and the order in which you will do them. Your answers don't have to be in the same order as the questions. If you think you have lots of time, it's a good idea to place your best answer first, your worst answers in the middle, and your second best answer at the end, in order to leave the reader on a high note. If you think you will be rushed, though, it's wiser to work from best to worst. That way you will be sure to get all the marks you can on your good answers, and you won't have to cut a good answer short at the end.

Read each question carefully
As you turn to each question, read it again carefully and underline all the key words. The wording will probably suggest the number of parts

your answer should have; be sure you don't overlook anything (a common mistake when people are nervous). Since the verb used in the question is usually a guide for the approach to take in your answer, it's especially important that you interpret the key words in the question correctly. In Chapter 4 we summarized what you should do when you are faced with words like *explain, compare, discuss,* and so on; it's a good idea to review this list before you go to the exam.

Make notes
Before you even begin to organize your answer, jot down key ideas and information related to the topic on rough paper or the unlined pages of your answer book. These notes will save you the worry of forgetting something by the time you begin writing. Next, arrange those parts you want to use into a brief plan.

Be direct
Get to the points quickly and illustrate them frequently. In an exam, as opposed to a term paper, it's best to use a direct approach. Don't worry about composing a graceful introduction: simply state the main points that you are going to discuss, then get on with developing them. Remember that your paper will likely be one of many read and marked by someone who has to work quickly—the clearer your answers are, the better they will be received.

For each main point give the kind of specific details that will prove you really know the materials. General statements will show you are able to assimilate information, but they need examples to back them up.

Write legibly
Writing that's hard to read produces a cranky reader. When the marker has to struggle to decipher your ideas, you may get poorer results than you deserve. If your writing is not very legible, it's probably better to print.

Write on alternate lines
Writing on every other line will not only make your writing easier to read, but leave you space for changes and additions; you won't have to cover your paper with a lot of messy circles and arrows.

Keep to your time plan
Keep to your plan and don't skip any questions. Try to write something on each topic. Remember that it's easier to score half marks for a question you don't know much about than it is to score full marks for

one you could write pages on. If you find yourself running out of time on an answer and still haven't finished, summarize the remaining points and go on to the next question. Leave a large space between questions so that you can go back and add more if you have time. If you write a new ending, remember to cross out the old one — neatly.

Reread your answers

No matter how tired or fed up you are, reread your answers at the end, if there's time. Check especially for clarity of expression; try to get rid of confusing sentences and increase the logical connections between your ideas. Revisions that make answers easier to read are always worth the effort.

Multiple-choice examinations

Many students are terrified of multiple-choice exams. They worry that they will need minutely detailed knowledge, or that the questions will be ambiguous. In some cases this is true, but often the problem lies in the students' test-taking strategies. Fleet, Goodchild, and Zajchowski (1994) outline a deliberate exam-writing procedure:

1. Read the *question* (not the answers) twice to get:
   (a) concepts
   (b) context (What does the question want you to do? You may need to translate the question into your own words).
2. Recall the appropriate conceptual information and try to think of the correct answer.
3. Now (and only now) read each alternative carefully. Again, you may need to translate the answers into your own words. Choose the one that best answers the meaning of the question. With luck, this will agree with the answer that you have generated yourself.
4. If there is no penalty for guessing, be sure to answer all the questions. It's unlikely that all your choices will be made at random, so you have a chance here to gain some extra points.
5. When you go back to look over your paper after answering all the questions you can, don't change any answers unless you are very sure; "second guesses" are often wrong.

Open-book examinations

If you think that permission to take your books into the exam room is a guarantee of success, be forewarned. You could fall into the trap of relying too heavily on them; you may spend so much time flipping through pages and looking things up that you won't have time to write good answers. The result may be worse than if you had been allowed no books at all.

If you want to do well, use your books only to check information and look up specific, hard-to-remember details for a topic you already know a good deal about. For instance, if your subject is biochemistry, you can look up chemical formulae; if it is statistics, you can look up equations; if it is psychology, you can look up specific terms or experimental details. In other words, use the books to make sure your answers are precise and well illustrated. Never use them to replace studying and careful exam preparation.

Take-home examinations

The benefit of a take-home exam is that you have time to plan your answers and to consult your texts or other sources. The catch is that the time is usually less than it would be for an ordinary essay. Don't work yourself into a frenzy trying to respond with a polished research essay for each question. Keep in mind that you were given this assignment to test your overall command of the course: your reader is likely to be less concerned with your specialized research than with evidence that you have understood and assimilated the material.

The guidelines for a take-home exam are similar to those for a regular exam; the only difference is that you don't need to keep such a close eye on the clock:

1. Keep your introduction short and get to the point quickly.
2. Have a straightforward and obvious organizational pattern so that the reader can easily see your main ideas.
3. Use concrete examples often to back up your points.
4. Where possible, show the range of your knowledge of course material by referring to a variety of sources, rather than constantly using the same ones.
5. Try to show that you can analyze and evaluate material: that you can do more than simply repeat information.

Reference
Fleet, J., Goodchild, F., & Zajchowski, R. (1994). *Learning for success: Skills and strategies for Canadian students* (Rev. ed.). Toronto: Harcourt Brace Canada.

11

Common errors in grammar

and usage

This chapter is not a comprehensive grammar lesson: it's simply a survey of those areas where students most often make mistakes. It will help you keep a look-out for weaknesses as you are editing your work. Once you get into the habit of checking, it won't be long before you are correcting potential problems as you write.

The grammatical terms used here are the most simple and familiar ones; if you need to review some of them, see the glossary. For a thorough treatment of grammar or usage see Thompson & Martinet (1980).

Troubles with sentence unity

Sentence fragments

To be complete, a sentence must have both a subject and a verb in an independent clause; if it doesn't, it's a fragment. There are times in informal writing when a sentence fragment is acceptable to emphasize a point, as in:

✓ What is the probability of contracting AIDS through casual contact? Very low.

Here the sentence fragment *Very low* is clearly intended to be understood as a short form of *The probability is very low.* Unintentional sentence fragments, on the other hand, usually seem incomplete rather than shortened:

✗ The liquid was poured into a glass beaker. Being a strong acid.

The last "sentence" is incomplete because it has no subject or verb. (Remember that a participle such as *being* is a verbal, not a verb.) The sentence can be made complete by adding a subject and a verb:

✓ The liquid was a strong acid.

Alternatively, you could join the fragment to the preceding sentence:

✓ The liquid was poured into a glass beaker because it was a strong acid.

✓ Because the liquid was a strong acid, it was poured into a glass beaker.

Run-on sentences

A run-on sentence is one that continues beyond the point where it should have stopped:

✗ The subjects who took part in the experiment said they enjoyed participating, even though it lasted for two hours, and they all agreed to come back for a second session, which will probably take place after reading week.

The *and* should be dropped and a period or semicolon added after *hours*.

Another kind of run-on sentence is one in which two independent clauses (phrases that could stand by themselves as sentences) are joined incorrectly by a comma:

✗ The instructions called for 50 g of sugar to be added, we used fructose in our experiment.

This error is known as a *comma splice*. There are three ways of correcting it:

• by putting a period after *added* and starting a new sentence:

. . . to be added. We . . .

• by replacing the comma with a semicolon:

. . . to be added; we . . .

• by making one of the independent clauses subordinate to the other, so that it can't stand by itself:

✓ The instructions, which called for 50 g of sugar to be added, allowed us to use fructose in our experiment.

Contrary to what many people think, words such as *however*, *therefore*, and *thus* cannot be used to join independent clauses:

✗ Two of my friends started out in science, however they quickly decided they didn't like chemistry.

The mistake can be corrected by beginning a new sentence after *science* or (preferably) by putting a semicolon in the same place:

✓ Two of my friends started out in science; however, they decided not to take chemistry.

The only words that can be used to join independent clauses are the coordinating conjunctions—*and, or, nor, but, for, yet,* and *so*—and subordinating conjunctions such as *if, because, since, while, when, where, after, before,* and *until.*

Faulty predication

When the subject of a sentence is not connected grammatically to what follows (the predicate), the result is faulty predication:

✗ The reason he failed was because he couldn't handle multiple-choice exams.

The problem is that *because* means essentially the same thing as *the reason for*. The subject needs a noun clause to complete it:

✓ The reason he failed was that he couldn't handle multiple-choice exams.

Another solution would be to rephrase the sentence:

✓ He failed because he couldn't handle multiple-choice exams.

Faulty *is when* or *is where* constructions can be corrected in the same way:

✗ The difficulty is when the two sets of data disagree.

✓ The difficulty arises when the two sets of data disagree.

Troubles with subject-verb agreement

Identifying the subject

A verb should always agree in number with its subject. Sometimes, however, when the subject does not come at the beginning of the sentence, or when it is separated from the verb by other information, you may be tempted to use a verb form that does not agree:

✗ The changes in the viscosity and the rate of flow was measured by the investigators.

The subject here is *changes*, not *rate of flow*; therefore the verb should be the plural *were measured*.

✓ The changes in the viscosity and the rate of flow were measured by the investigators.

Either, neither, each

The indefinite pronouns *either*, *neither*, and *each* always take singular verbs:

✗   Neither of the cats <u>have</u> a flea collar.

✓   <u>Each</u> of them <u>has</u> a rabies tag.

Compound subjects

When *or*, *either . . . or*, or *neither . . . nor* is used to create a compound subject, the verb should usually agree with the last item in the subject:

Neither the professor nor his <u>students were able</u> to solve the equation.

If a singular item follows a plural item, however, a singular verb may sound awkward, and it's better to rephrase the sentence:

orig · Either my history <u>books</u> or my biology <u>text is going</u> to gather dust this weekend.

rev.   This week, I'm going to leave behind either my history books or my biology text.

Unlike the word *and*, which creates a compound subject and therefore takes a plural verb, *as well as* or *in addition to* does not create a compound subject; therefore the verb remains singular:

✓   Organic chemistry <u>and</u> applied math <u>are</u> difficult subjects.

✓   Organic chemistry <u>as well as</u> applied math <u>is</u> a difficult subject.

Collective nouns

A collective noun is a singular noun, such as *family*, *army*, or *team*, that includes a number of members. If the noun refers to the members as a unit, it takes a singular verb:

✓   The <u>class goes</u> on a field trip in June.

If the noun refers to the members as individuals, however, the verb becomes plural:

✓   The <u>team are receiving</u> their prizes this week.

✓   The <u>majority</u> of bears <u>hibernate</u> in winter.

Titles

A title is singular even if it contains plural words; therefore it takes a singular verb:

✓ The Thirty Nine Steps is an interesting book.

✓ Bausch and Lomb is a company that makes microscopes.

Tense troubles

Native speakers of English usually know the correct sequence of verb tenses by ear, but a few tenses can still be confusing.

The past perfect

If the main verb is in the past tense and you want to refer to something before that time, use the past perfect (*had* plus the past participle). The time sequence will not be clear if you use the simple past in both clauses:

✗ He hoped that she bought the typewriter.

✓ He hoped that she had bought the typewriter.

Similarly, when you are reporting what someone said in the past — that is, when you are using past indirect discourse — you should use the past perfect tense in the clause describing what was said:

✗ He said that the party caused the neighbors to complain.

✓ He said that the party had caused the neighbors to complain.

Using "if"

When you are describing a possibility in the future, use the present tense in the condition (*if*) clause and the future tense in the consequence clause:

✓ If he tests us on operant conditioning, I will fail.

When the possibility is unlikely, it is conventional — especially in formal writing — to use the subjunctive in the *if* clause, and *would* plus the base verb in the consequence clause:

✓ If he were to cancel the test, I would cheer.

When you are describing a hypothetical instance in the past, use the past subjunctive (it has the same form as the past perfect) in the *if* clause and *would have* plus the past participle for the consequence. A common error is to use *would have* in both clauses:

✗ If he would have been more friendly, I would have asked him to be my lab partner.

✓ If he had been more friendly, I would have asked him to be my lab partner.

Pronoun troubles

Pronoun reference
The link between a pronoun and the noun it refers to must be clear. If the noun doesn't appear in the same sentence as the pronoun, it should appear in the preceding sentence:

✗ The textbook supply in the bookstore had run out, so we borrowed them from the library.

Because *textbook* is used as an adjective rather than a noun, it cannot serve as referent or antecedent for the pronoun *them*. You must either replace *them* or change the phrase *textbook supply*.

✓ The textbook supply in the bookstore had run out, so we borrowed the texts from the library.

✓ The textbooks in the bookstore had run out, and so we borrowed them from the library.

When a sentence contains more than one noun, make sure there is no ambiguity about which noun the pronoun refers to:

✗ The faculty want increased salaries as well as fewer teaching hours, but the administration does not favour them.

What does the pronoun *them* refer to? The salary increases, the reduced teaching hours, or both?

✓ The faculty want increased salaries as well as fewer teaching hours, but the administration does not favour pay raises.

Using "it" and "this"
Using *it* and *this* without a clear referent can lead to confusion:

✗ Although the directors wanted to meet in January, it (this) didn't take place until May.

✓ Although the directors wanted to meet in January, the conference didn't take place until May.

Make sure that *it* or *this* clearly refers to a specific noun or pronoun.

Pronoun agreement
A pronoun should agree in number and person with the noun that it refers to:

✗ When a student is sick, their class-mates usually help out.

✓ When a student is sick, his class-mates usually help out.

Traditionally, the word *his* has been used to indicate both male and female, and most grammarians still maintain that *his* is the correct form. If you feel uncomfortable about using *his* alone, or want to avoid charges of sexism, now and again you may resort to the more cumbersome *his or her*, as this handbook occasionally does. Where possible, though, it's better to try switching from the singular to the plural in both noun and pronoun:

✔ When <u>students</u> are sick, <u>their</u> class-mates usually help out.

Using "one"
People often use the word *one* to avoid over-using *I* in their writing. Although in Britain this is common, in Canada and the United States frequent use of *one* may seem too formal and even a bit pompous:

If <u>one</u> were to apply for the grant, <u>one</u> would find oneself engulfed in so many bureaucratic forms that <u>one's</u> patience would be stretched thin.

As a way out, it's becoming increasingly common in North America to use the third-person *his* or *her* as the adjectival form of *one*:

<u>One</u> would find <u>his</u> patience stretched thin.

In any case, try to use *one* sparingly, and don't be afraid of the occasional *I*. The one serious error to avoid is mixing the third-person *one* with the second-person *you*.

✗ When <u>one</u> visits the cyclotron, <u>you</u> are impressed by its size.

In formal academic writing generally, *you* is not an appropriate substitute for *one*.

Using "me" and other objective pronouns
Remembering that it's wrong to say "Jane and me were invited to the party," rather than "Jane and I were invited," many people use the subjective form of the pronoun even when it should be objective:

✗ He invited Jane and <u>I</u> to the party.

✔ He invited Jane and <u>me</u> to the party.

A good way to tell which form is correct is to ask yourself how the sentence would sound if the pronoun were used by itself. It will be obvious that the subjective form—"He invited I . . ."—is not appropriate.

The verb *invited* requires an object; *me* is the objective case. The same problem often arises following a preposition:

✗ Between <u>you</u> and <u>I</u>, this result doesn't make sense.

✔ Between <u>you</u> and <u>me</u>, this result doesn't make sense.

✗ Eating well is a problem <u>for we</u> students.

✓ Eating well is a problem <u>for us</u> students.

There are times, however, when the correct case can sound stiff or awkward:

orig. To whom was the award given?

Instead of keeping to a correct but awkward form, try to reword the sentence:

rev. Who received the award?

Exceptions for pronouns following prepositions

The rule that a pronoun following a preposition takes the objective case has exceptions. When the preposition is followed by a clause, the pronoun should take the case required by its position in the clause:

✗ The Chair showed some concern about <u>whom would be selected as Dean.</u>

Although the pronoun follows the preposition *over*, it is also the subject of the verb *would be selected* and therefore requires the subjective case:

✓ The Chair showed some concern about <u>who would be selected as Dean.</u>

Similarly, when a gerund (a word that acts partly as a noun and partly as a verb) is the subject of a clause, the pronoun that modifies it takes the possessive case:

✗ We were surprised by <u>him dropping</u> out of school.

✓ We were surprised by <u>his dropping</u> out of school.

Troubles with modifying

Adjectives modify nouns; adverbs modify verbs, adjectives, and other adverbs. Do not use an adjective to modify a verb:

✗ He played <u>good</u>. (Adjective with verb)

✓ He played <u>well</u>. (Adverb modifying verb)

✓ He played <u>really well</u>. (Adverb modifying adverb)

✓ He had a <u>good style</u>. (Adjective modifying noun)

✓ He had a <u>really good</u> style. (Adverb modifying adjective)

Squinting modifiers

Remember that clarity depends on word order: to avoid confusion, the relations between the different parts of a sentence must be clear. Modifiers should therefore be as close as possible to the words they modify. A squinting modifier is one that, because of its position, seems to look in two directions at once:

> X   She discovered <u>in the spring</u> she was going to have to write her final exams.

Was spring the time of the discovery or the time of the exams? The logical relation is usually clearest when you place the modifier immediately before or after the element it modifies:

> ✓   <u>In the spring</u> she <u>discovered</u> that she was going to have to write her final exams.

> ✓   She discovered that she would have to write her <u>final exams in the spring</u>.

Other squinting modifiers can be corrected in the same way:

> X   Our biology professor gave a lecture on <u>Planaria</u>, <u>which was well-illustrated</u>.

> ✓   Our biology professor gave a <u>well-illustrated lecture</u> on <u>Planaria</u>.

Dangling modifiers

Modifiers that have no grammatical connection with anything else in the sentence are said to be dangling:

> X   <u>Walking</u> around the campus in June, the river and trees made a picturesque scene.

Who is doing the walking? Here's another example:

> X   <u>Reflecting</u> on the results of the study, it was decided not to submit the paper for publication.

Who is doing the reflecting? Clarify the meaning by connecting the dangling modifier to a new subject:

> ✓   <u>Walking</u> around the campus in June, <u>she</u> thought the river and trees made a picturesque scene.

> ✓   <u>Reflecting</u> on the results of the study, <u>they</u> decided not to submit the paper for publication.

Troubles with pairs (and more)

Comparisons

Make sure that your comparisons are complete. The second element in a comparison should be equivalent to the first, whether the equivalent is stated or merely implied.

✗ Today's students have a greater understanding of calculus than their parents.

The sentence suggests that the two things being compared are calculus and parents. Adding a second verb (*have*) equivalent to the first one shows that the two things being compared are parents' understanding and students' understanding:

✓ Today's students have a greater understanding of calculus than their parents have.

A similar problem arises in the following comparison:

✗ The new text is a boring book and so are the lectures.

The lectures may be boring, but they are not *a boring book*; to make sense, the two parts of the comparison must be parallel:

✓ The new text is boring and so are the lectures.

Correlatives (coordinate constructions)

Constructions such as *both . . . and, not only . . . but,* and *neither . . . nor* are especially tricky. The coordinating term must not come too early, or else one of the parts that come after will not connect with the common element. For the implied comparison to work, the two parts that come after the coordinating term must be grammatically equivalent:

✗ He not only studies music but math.

✓ He studies not only music but math.

Parallel phrasing

A series of items in a sentence should be phrased in parallel wording. Make sure that all the parts of a parallel construction are really equal:

✗ We had to turn in our rough notes, our calculations and finished assignment.

✓ We had to turn in our rough notes, our calculations and our finished assignment.

Once you have decided to include the pronoun *our* in the first two elements, the third must have it too.

For clarity as well as stylistic grace, keep similar ideas in similar form:

✗ He failed Genetics and barely passed Statistics, but Zoology was a subject he did well in.

✓ He failed Genetics and barely passed Statistics, but did well in Zoology.

Reference

Thompson, A.J., & Martinet, A.V. (1980). *A practical English grammar* (3rd. ed.). Oxford, England: Oxford University Press.

12

Punctuation

Punctuation causes students so many problems that it deserves a chapter of its own. If your punctuation is faulty, your readers will be confused and may have to backtrack; worse still, they may be tempted to skip over the rough spots. Punctuation marks are the traffic signals of writing; use them with precision to keep readers moving smoothly through your work. Most of the rules we give below are general, but when there were several possibilities (for example, when British and American usages differ), we have used the APA style guidelines.

Period [.]

1. Use a period at the end of a sentence. A period indicates a full stop, not just a pause.

2. Use a period with abbreviations. This includes initials, place-names (B.C., N.W.T.), and abbreviated titles (Ms., Dr.). However, you do not need a period for U.S. state abbreviations (MA, OH) or for capital-letter abbreviations and acronyms (APA, CARE, CIDA).

3. Use a period at the end of an indirect question. Do *not* use a question mark:

   X   He asked if I wanted a clean lab coat?

   ✓   He asked if I wanted a clean lab coat.

Comma [,]

Commas are the trickiest of all punctuation marks: even the experts differ on when to use them. Most agree, however, that too many commas are as bad as too few, since they make writing choppy and awkward to read. Certainly recent writers use fewer commas than earlier writers did. Whenever you are in doubt, let clarity be your guide. The most widely accepted conventions are these:

1. Use a comma to separate two independent clauses joined by a coordinating conjunction (and, but, for, or, nor, yet, so). By signalling that there are two clauses, the comma will prevent the reader from confusing the beginning of the second clause with the end of the first:

> X He finished working with the microscope and his partner turned off the power.

> ✓ He finished working with the microscope, and his partner turned off the power.

When the second clause has the same subject as the first, you have the option of omitting both the second subject and the comma:

> ✓ He writes well, but he never finishes on time.

> ✓ He writes well but never finishes on time.

If you mistakenly punctuate two sentences as if they were one, the result will be a run-on sentence; if you use a comma but forget the coordinating conjunction, the result will be a comma splice:

> X He took his class to the zoo, it was closed for repairs.

> ✓ He took his class to the zoo, but it was closed for repairs.

Remember that words such as *however, therefore,* and *thus* are conjunctive adverbs, not conjunctions: if you use one of them the way you would use a conjunction, the result will again be a comma splice:

> X She was accepted into medical school, however, she took a year off to earn her tuition.

> ✓ She was accepted into medical school; however, she took a year off to earn her tuition.

Conjunctive adverbs are often confused with conjunctions. You can distinguish between the two if you remember that a conjunctive adverb's position in a sentence can be changed:

> ✓ She was accepted into medical school; she took a year off, however, to earn her tuition.

The position of a conjunction, on the other hand, is invariable; it must be placed between the two clauses:

✓ She was accepted into medical school, <u>but</u> she took a year off to earn her tuition.

When, in rare cases, the independent clauses are short and closely related, they may be joined by a comma alone:

✓ I came, I saw, I conquered.

A fused sentence is a run-on sentence in which independent clauses are slapped together with no punctuation at all:

✗ He watched the hockey game all afternoon the only exercise he got was going to the kitchen between periods.

A fused sentence sounds like breathless babbling—and it's a serious error.

2. Use a comma between items in a series. (Place a coordinating conjunction before the last item):

✓ The room that housed the animals was large, bright, and clean.

✓ There is a cage-washer, bottle-washer, and a place for storing the clean glassware.

The comma before the conjunction is optional:

✓ We have an office, a lab and a surgery.

Sometimes, however, the final comma can help to prevent confusion:

✓ We arranged to move the rats, photographs of the lab, and the gerbil food.

In this case, the comma prevents the reader from thinking that *photographs* refers both to the lab and to the gerbil food.

3. Use a comma to separate adjectives preceding a noun when they modify the same element:

✓ It was a reliable, accurate weighing device.

When the adjectives do not modify the same element, however, you should not use a comma:

✓ It was an expensive chemical balance.

Here *chemical* modifies *balance* but *expensive* modifies the total phrase *chemical balance*. A good way of checking whether or not you need a comma is to see if you can reverse the order of the adjectives. If you can reverse it (*reliable, accurate balance* or *accurate, reliable balance*), use a comma; if you can't (*chemical expensive balance*), omit the comma.

4. Use commas to set off an interruption (an interrupting word or phrase is technically called a parenthetical element):

✓ The outcome, he said, was a complete failure.

✓ My tutor, however, couldn't answer the question.

Remember to put commas on both sides of the interruption:

✗ The equipment, they reported was obsolete.

✓ The equipment, they reported, was obsolete.

5. Use commas to set off words or phrases that provide additional but non-essential information:

✓ Her grade in statistics, her favourite course, was not very high.

✓ The new computer, his pride and joy, was always crashing.

Her favourite course and *his pride and joy* are appositives: they give additional information about the nouns they refer to (*statistics* and *computer*), but the sentences would be understandable without them. Here's another example:

✓ Equinox magazine, which is published locally, often contains material that I can use in my course.

The phrase *which is published locally* is called a non-restrictive modifier, because it does not limit the meaning of the words it modifies (*Equinox magazine*). Without that modifying clause the sentence would still refer to the contents of the magazine. Since the information the clause provides is not necessary to the meaning of the sentence, you must use commas on both sides to set it off.

In contrast, a restrictive modifier is one that provides essential information; therefore it must not be set apart from the element it modifies, and commas should not be used:

✓ The magazine that has the black cover is Equinox.

Without the clause *that has the black cover* the reader would not know which magazine was *Equinox*.

To avoid confusion, be sure to distinguish carefully between essential and additional information. The difference can be important:

Students who are not willing to work should not receive grants.

Students, who are not willing to work, should not receive grants.

6. Use a comma after an introductory phrase when omitting it would cause confusion:

✗ In the room behind the students flew paper airplanes.

✓ In the room behind, the students flew paper airplanes.

7. Use a comma to separate elements in dates, addresses, and years:

February 2, 1993. (Commas are often omitted if the day comes first: 2 February 1993)

117 Hudson Drive, Edmonton, Alberta.

They lived in Dartmouth, Nova Scotia.

8. Use a comma before a quotation in a sentence:

He stated, "E. coli was the bacterium isolated."

"The most difficult part of the procedure," he reported, "was finding the material to work with."

For more formality, you may use a colon (see p. 110).

9. Use a comma with a name followed by a title:

D. Gunn, Ph.D.

Alice Smith, M.D.

Semicolon [;]

1. Use a semicolon to join independent clauses (complete sentences) that are closely related:

For five days he worked non-stop; by Saturday he was exhausted.

His lecture was confusing; no one could understand the terminology.

A semicolon is especially useful when the second independent clause begins with a conjunctive adverb such as *however, moreover, consequently, nevertheless, in addition,* or *therefore* (usually followed by a comma):

He made several attempts; however, none of them was successful.

Some grammarians may disagree, but it's usually acceptable to follow a semicolon with a coordinating conjunction if the second clause is complicated by other commas:

> Some of these animals, wolverine and lynx in particular, are rarely seen; but occasionally, if you are patient, you might catch a glimpse of one.

2. Use a semicolon to mark the divisions in a complicated series when individual items themselves need commas. Using a comma to mark the subdivisions and a semicolon to mark the main divisions will help to prevent mix-ups:

> X He invited Prof. Brooks, the vice-principal, Jane Hunter, and John Taylor.

Is the vice-principal a separate person?

> ✓ He invited Prof. Brooks, the vice-principal; Jane Hunter; and John Taylor.

In a case such as this, the elements separated by the semicolon need not be independent clauses.

Colon [:]

A colon indicates that something is to follow.

1. Use a colon before a formal statement or series:

> The layers are the following: sclera, choroid, and retina.

Do not use a colon if the words preceding it do not form a complete sentence:

> X The layers are: sclera, choroid, and retina.
> ✓ The layers are sclera, choroid, and retina.

2. Use a colon for formality before a direct quotation:

> The instructor was adamant: "All students must take the exam today."

Dash [—]

A dash creates an abrupt pause, emphasizing the words that follow. (Never use dashes as casual substitutes for other punctuation: overuse can detract from the calm, well-reasoned effect you want.)

1. Use a dash to stress a word or phrase:

The fire alarm—which was deafening—warned them of the danger.

I thought that writing this paper would be easy—when I started.

2. Use a dash in interrupted or unfinished dialogue:

"It's a matter—to put it delicately—of personal hygiene."

In typing, use two hyphens together, with no spaces on either side, to show a dash.

Exclamation mark [!]

An exclamation mark helps to show emotion or feeling. In scientific writing, there is virtually no time when you would need to use it.

Quotation marks [" " or ' ']

Quotation marks are used for several purposes, as described below. Conventions regarding single or double marks vary, but APA style recommends that you use double marks for quotations within the running text and single for quotations within quotations.

1. Use quotation marks to signify direct discourse (the actual words of a speaker):

I asked, "What is the matter?"
He said, "I have a pain in my big toe."

2. Use quotation marks to show that words themselves are the issue:

The term "information processing" has a distinct meaning in psychology.

Alternatively, you may italicize or underline the terms in question.

Sometimes quotation marks are used to mark a slang word or an inappropriate usage, to show that the writer is aware of the difficulty:

Several of the "experts" did not seem to know anything about the topic.

Use this device only when necessary; usually it's better to let the context show your attitude, or to choose another term.

3. Use single quotation marks to enclose quotations within quotations:

> He said, "Several of the 'experts' did not seem to know anything about the topic."

Placement of punctuation with quotation marks

The *APA manual* suggests a simple rule for where punctuation marks should go with respect to quotation marks: periods and commas always go inside closing quotation marks; other punctuation marks go outside unless they are part of the quoted material. With a block quotation (one that is set off from the running text), you do not need to use any quotation marks, but for quotations within the block use double quotation marks.

Apostrophe [']

The apostrophe forms the possessive case for nouns and some pronouns.

1. Add an apostrophe followed by "s" to:
- all singular and plural nouns not ending in s: *cat's, women's.*
- singular *proper* nouns ending in s: *Willis's, Collins's* (but note that the final *s* can be omitted if the word has a number of them already and would sound awkward, as in *Aloysius'*).
- indefinite pronouns: *someone's, anybody's,* etc;

2. Add an apostrophe to plural nouns ending in "s": *families', species', frogs'.*

Parentheses [( )]

1. Use parentheses to enclose an explanation, example, or qualification. Parentheses show that the enclosed material is of incidental importance to the main idea. They make a less pronounced interruption than a dash, but a more pronounced one than a comma:

> The meerkat (a mongoose-like animal) is found in Southern Africa.

> At least thirty people (according to the newspaper report) were under observation.

Remember that although punctuation should not precede parentheses, it may follow them if required by the sense of the sentence:

> There were some complaints (mainly from the less experienced students), but we decided to continue with the project anyway.

If the parenthetical statement comes between two complete sentences, it should be punctuated as a sentence, with the period inside the parentheses:

> I finished my last essay on April 3. (It was on long-term memory.) Fortunately, I had three weeks free to study for the exam.

2. Use parentheses to enclose reference citations. See Chapter 8 for details.

Brackets [ ]

Brackets are square enclosures, not to be confused with parentheses (which are round).

1. Use brackets to set off a remark of your own within a quotation. They show that the words enclosed are not those of the person quoted:

> Mitchell (1984) stated, "Several of the changes observed [in the cat] are seen also in the monkey."

Brackets are sometimes used to enclose *sic* (Latin for *thus*), which is used after an error, such as a misspelling, to show that the mistake was in the original. *Sic* should always be underlined:

> In describing the inhabitants of a tidal pool, he wrote that "it was almost impossible to loosen barnikles [sic] from the rock surface."

Hyphen [-]

1. Use a hyphen if you must divide a word at the end of a line. When a word is too long to fit at the end of a line, it's best to keep it in one piece by starting a new line. But if you must divide, remember these rules:

- Divide between syllables.
- Never divide a one-syllable word.
- Never leave one letter by itself.
- Divide double consonants except when they come before a suffix, in which case divide before the suffix:

    ar-rangement
    embar-rassment
    fall-ing
    pass-able

When the second consonant has been added to form the suffix, keep it with the suffix:

    refer-ral
    begin-ning

2. Use a hyphen to separate the parts of certain compound words:

compound nouns: test-tube, vice-president
compound verbs: fine-tune, proof-read
compound adjectives used as modifiers preceding nouns:
    well-designed study, sixteenth-century science

When you are not using such expressions adjectivally, do not hyphenate them:

    The study was well designed.

    It dates from the sixteenth century.

After long-time use, some compound nouns drop the hyphen. When in doubt, check a dictionary.

3. Use a hyphen with certain prefixes (*all-*, *self-*, *ex-*, and those prefixes preceding a proper name):

    all-trans retinal, self-imposed, ex-student, pro-nuclear

4. Use a hyphen to emphasize contrasting prefixes:

    Both pre- and post-treatment measures were taken.

5. Use a hyphen to separate written-out compound numbers from one to a hundred and compound fractions used as modifiers: Remember that numbers above nine are written out only when they begin a sentence:

Eighty-one centimetres

seven-tenths full

6. Use a hyphen to separate parts of inclusive numbers or dates:

the years 1973-1976

pages 3-40

Ellipsis [. . .]

1. Use an ellipsis to show an omission from a quotation:

"The hormonal control of reproduction is modulated . . . ultimately by the production of gonadal steroids."

If the omission comes at the end of a sentence, include the original period (without a space) before the ellipsis.

2. Use an ellipsis to show that a series of numbers continues indefinitely:

1,3,5,7,9 . . .

Italics [*italics*] and <u>underlining</u>

Italics are slanted (cursive) letters. If you use a typewriter that can't produce italics, underlining is an acceptable substitute. As we mentioned earlier, APA manuscript style requires that you use underlining for material that will be typeset in italics. There are several occasions when you would want to use italics:

1. Titles of books and periodicals:

Darwin's <u>Origin of Species</u>.

2. Biological names:

<u>Rattus norvegicus</u>

3. When a word or phrase is used as a linguistic example:

They were asked to solve an anagram of the word <u>photography</u>.

4. Words that could be misread or misunderstood:

the <u>aging</u> professors (those studying older people)

5. Letters used as symbols or algebraic terms:

<u>SD</u> (standard deviation)

<u>df</u> = 17 (degrees of freedom)

You can also use italics for emphasizing a word or an idea. However, you should not do this too often, or the emphasis will lose its power.

Catchlist of misused

words and phrases

accept, except. Accept is a verb meaning to *receive affirmatively*; **except**, when used as a verb, means to *exclude*:

> I accept your offer.
> The teacher excepted him from the general punishment.

accompanied by, accompanied with. Use **accompanied by** for people; **accompanied with** for objects:

> He was accompanied by his wife.
> The brochure arrived, accompanied with a discount coupon.

advice, advise. Advice is a noun, **advise** a verb:

> He was advised to ignore the others' advice.

affect, effect. As a verb to **affect** means to *influence*; as a noun it's a technical psychological term. The verb to **effect** means to *bring about*. The noun means *result*. In most cases, you will be safe if you remember to use **affect** for the verb and **effect** for the noun:

> The eye drops affect his vision.
> The effect of higher government spending is higher inflation.

alright. Always spell as two words: **all right**.

alternately, alternatively. Use **alternately** when you mean "in turn"; use **alternatively** when you mean "providing a choice or alternative."

> When she addressed the crowd, she turned alternately to her left and her right.
> Alternatively, we can choose the less expensive printer.

all together, altogether. All together means *in a group*; **altogether** is an adverb meaning *entirely*:

He was altogether certain that the children were all together.

allusion, illusion. An **allusion** is an indirect reference to something; an **illusion** is a false perception:

The rock image is an allusion to the myth of Sisyphus.
He thought he saw a sea monster, but it was an illusion.

alot. Write as two separate words: *a lot*.

among, between. Use **among** for three or more persons or objects, **between** for two:

Between you and me, there's trouble among the team members.

amoral, immoral. **Amoral** means *non-moral* or outside the moral sphere; **immoral** means *wicked*:

As an art critic, he was amoral in his judgements.
That immoral performance should be restricted to adults.

amount, number. Use **amount** for money or non-countable quantities; use **number** for countable items:

No amount of wealth or number of expensive possessions will make up for a lack of love.

anyways. Non-standard English: use *anyway*.

as, because. **As** is a weaker conjunction than **because** and may be confused with *when*:

X As I was working, I ate at my desk.
✓ Because I was working, I ate at my desk.

X He arrived as I was leaving.
✓ He arrived when I was leaving.

as to. A common feature of bureaucratese; replace it with a single-word preposition such as *about* or *on*:

X They were concerned as to the range of disagreement.
✓ They were concerned about the range of disagreement.

X They recorded his comments as to the treaty.
✓ They recorded his comments on the treaty.

bad, badly. **Bad** is an adjective meaning *not good*:

The meat tastes bad.
He felt bad about forgetting the dinner party.

Badly is an adverb meaning *not well*; when used with the verbs **want** or **need**, it means *very much*:

> She thought he played the villain's part badly.
> I badly need a new suit.

beside, besides. Beside is a preposition meaning *next to*:

> She worked beside her assistant.

Besides has two uses: as a preposition it means *in addition to*; as a conjunctive adverb it means *moreover*:

> Besides recommending the changes, the consultants are implementing them.
> Besides, it was hot and we wanted to rest.

between. See **among.**

bring, take. One **brings** something to a closer place and **takes** it to a farther one.

can, may. Can means to *be able*; **may** means to *have permission*:

> Can you fix the lock?
> May I have another piece of cake?

In speech, **can** is used to cover both meanings; in formal writing, however, you should observe the distinction.

can't hardly. A faulty combination of the phrases **can't** and **can hardly.** Use one or the other of them instead:

> He can't swim.
> He can hardly swim.

capital, capitol. As a noun **capital** may refer to a seat of government, the top of a pillar, an upper-case letter, or accumulated wealth. **Capitol** refers only to a specific American — or ancient Roman — legislative building.

complement, compliment. The verb to **complement** means to *complete*; to **compliment** means to *praise*.

> His engineering skill complements the skills of the designers.
> I complimented her on her outstanding report.

comprise, include. Comprise refers to all the parts of something, whereas **include** refers to some of them. Avoid the phrase "is comprised of."

> My class comprises twenty men and eighteen women; for the first time, it includes four exchange students from China.

continual, continuous. Continual means *repeated over a period of time*; **continuous** means *constant* or *without interruption*:

> The strikes caused continual delays in building the road.
> In August, it rained continuously for five days.

could of. Incorrect, as are **might of**, **should of**, and **would of**. Replace *of* with *have*.

> ✗ He could of done it.
> ✓ He could have done it.
> ✓ They might have been there.
> ✓ I should have known.
> ✓ We would have left earlier.

council, counsel. Council is a noun meaning an *advisory* or *deliberative assembly*. **Counsel** as a noun means *advice* or *lawyer*; as a verb it means to *give advice*.

> The college council meets on Tuesday.
> We respect his counsel, since he's seldom wrong.
> As a camp counsellor, you may need to counsel parents as well as children.

criterion, criteria. A **criterion** is a standard for judging something. **Criteria** is the plural of **criterion** and thus requires a plural verb:

> These are my criteria for selecting the paintings.

data. The plural of *datum*, **data** is increasingly treated as a singular noun, but this usage is not yet acceptable in formal prose: use a plural verb.

different than. Incorrect. Use either **different from** (American usage) or **different to** (British).

disinterested, uninterested. Disinterested implies impartiality or neutrality; **uninterested** implies a lack of interest:

> As a disinterested observer, he was in a good position to judge the issue fairly.
> Uninterested in the proceedings, he yawned repeatedly.

due to. Although increasingly used to mean *because of*, **due** is an adjective and therefore needs to modify something:

> ✗ Due to his impatience, we lost the contract. [Due is dangling]
> ✓ The loss was due to his impatience.

farther, further. Farther refers to distance, **further** to extent:

> He paddled farther than his friends.
> He explained the plan further.

good, well. Good is an adjective, not a verb. **Well** can be both: as an adverb, it means *effectively*; as an adjective, it means *healthy*:

> The pear sauce tastes good.
> She is a good golfer.
> She plays golf well.
> At last, he is well again after his long bout of flu.

hanged, hung. Hanged means *executed by hanging*. **Hung** means *suspended* or *clung to*:

> He was hanged at dawn for the murder.
> He hung the picture.
> He hung to the boat when it capsized.

hopefully. Use **hopefully** as an adverb meaning *full of hope*:

> She scanned the horizon hopefully, waiting for her friend's ship to appear.

In formal writing, using **hopefully** to mean *I hope* is still frowned upon, although increasingly common; it's better to use *I hope*:

> ✗ Hopefully we'll make a bigger profit this year.
> ✓ I hope we'll make a bigger profit this year.

imply, infer. Imply refers to what a statement suggests; **infer** relates to the audience's interpretation:

> His letter implied that he was lonely.
> I inferred from his letter that he would welcome a visit.

irregardless. Redundant; use *regardless*.

its, it's. Its is a form of possessive pronoun; **it's** is a contraction of *it is*. Many people mistakenly put an apostrophe in **its** in order to show possession.

> ✗ The cub wanted it's mother.
> ✓ The cub wanted its mother.
> ✓ It's time to leave.

lead, led. Unlike the verb *read*, which does not change its spelling to form the past tense, the verb **lead** changes both its pronunciation and its spelling:

The path leads through the forest.
Isabel led the way.

less, fewer. Use **less** for money and things that are not countable; use **fewer** for things that are:

Now that he's earning less money he's going to fewer movies.

lie, lay. To **lie** means to *assume a horizontal position*; to **lay** means to *put down.* The changes of tense often cause confusion:

Present	Past	Past participle
lie	lay	lain
lay	laid	laid

Remember that a person who is tired should "lie down", not "lay down."

like, as. **Like** is a preposition, but it is often wrongly used as a conjunction. To join two independent clauses, use the conjunction **as:**

✗ I want to progress like you have this year.
✓ I want to progress as you have this year.
✓ Prof. Dodd is like my old school principal.

literally. This means *exactly as stated.* It does not mean *figuratively.*

✗ I'm literally suffocating in this stuffy room.
✓ Such a sustained loud noise can literally damage the ears.

media. The plural of **medium.** Do not use as a singular noun:

The most effective medium for advertising is television.
Of the three media available, television is the most effective.

might of. See **could of.**

momentarily. This word means *for a brief time.* When you mean *very soon,* use *presently.*

✗ The game will resume momentarily.
✓ The game will resume presently.
✓ The speaker has been delayed momentarily but will presently appear.

myself, me. **Myself** is an intensifier of, not a substitute for, *I* or *me:*

✗ He gave it to John and myself.
✓ He gave it to John and me.

✗ Jane and myself are invited.
✓ Jane and I are invited.

✓ <u>Myself</u>, I would prefer a swivel chair.

nor, or. Use **nor** with **neither** and **or** by itself or with **either**:

He is <u>neither</u> overworked <u>nor</u> underfed.
The plant is <u>either</u> diseased <u>or</u> dried out.

nuclear. Note the spelling; often mispronounced as "nucular."

off of. Remove the unnecessary **of**:

The fence kept the children <u>off of</u> the premises.
The fence kept the children <u>off</u> the premises.

phenomenon. A singular noun: the plural is **phenomena**.

principal, principle. As an adjective, **principal** means *main* or *most important*; a **principal** is the *head of a school*. A **principle** is a *law* or *controlling idea*:

Our <u>principal</u> aim is to reduce the deficit.
Our <u>principal</u>, Prof. Smart, retires next year.
We are defending the island as a matter of <u>principle</u>.

rational, rationale. **Rational** is an adjective meaning *logical* or *able to reason*. **Rationale** is a noun meaning *explanation*:

That was not a <u>rational</u> decision.
The president sent around a memo with a <u>rationale</u> for his proposal.

real, really. The adjective **real** should never be used as an adverb; use *really* instead:

✓ We had <u>real</u> maple syrup with our pancakes.
✗ It was <u>real</u> good.
✓ It was <u>really</u> good.

set, sit. To **sit** means to *rest on the buttocks*; to **set** means to *put* or *place*:

After standing so long, you'll want to <u>sit</u> down.
Please <u>set</u> the bowl on the table.

should of. See **could of**.

their, there. **Their** is the possessive form of the third-person plural pronoun. **There** is usually an adverb, meaning *at that place* or *at that point*; sometimes it is used as an expletive (an introductory word in a sentence):

They parked <u>their</u> bikes <u>there</u>.
<u>There</u> is no point in arguing with you.

thus. A conjunctive adverb (see p. 106). Can be used to link an independent clause and a verbal phrase, but not two independent clauses:

✔ He hung up, thus ending the discussion.
✘ He hung up, thus he ended the discussion.
✔ He hung up; thus he ended the discussion.

to, too, two. **To** is a preposition, as well as part of the infinitive form of a verb:

We went to town in order to shop.

Too is an adjective showing degree (the soup is *too* hot) or an adverb meaning *moreover*. **Two** is the spelled version of the number 2.

while. To avoid misreading, use **while** only when you mean *at the same time that*. Do not use it as a substitute for *although*, *whereas*, or *but*:

✘ While he's getting fair marks, he'd like to do better.
✘ I headed for home, while she decided to stay.
✔ He fell asleep while he was reading.

-wise. Never use **-wise** as a suffix to form new words when you mean *with regard to*:

✘ Sales-wise, the company did better last year.
✔ With regard to sales, the company did better last year.

(or)

✔ The company's sales increased last year.

would have, would of. When people are describing a hypothetical instance in the past, they often mistakenly use **would have** in both the condition (*if*) clause and the consequence clause: see p. 98. For **would of**, see *could of*.

your, you're. **Your** is a pronominal adjective used to show possession; **you're** is a contraction of *you are*:

You're likely to miss your train.

Glossary

abstract
a summary accompanying a formal scientific report or paper, briefly outlining the contents.

abstract language
theoretical language removed from concrete particulars: e.g., *justice, goodness, truth* (cf. **concrete language**).

acronym
a word made up of the first letters of a group of words: e.g. *NATO* for *North Atlantic Treaty Organization*.

active voice
see **voice**.

adjective
a word that modifies or describes a noun or pronoun, hence a kind of noun marker: e.g., *red, beautiful, solemn*. An **adjectival phrase** or **adjectival clause** is a group of words modifying a noun or pronoun.

adverb
a word that modifies or qualifies a verb, adjective, or adverb, often answering a question such as *how? why? when?* or *where?*: e.g., *slowly, fortunately, early, abroad*. An **adverbial phrase** or **adverbial clause** is a group of words modifying a verb, adjective, or adverb: e.g., *by force, in revenge*. See also **conjunctive adverb**.

agreement
consistency in tense, number, or person between related parts of a sentence: e.g., between subject and verb, or noun and related pronoun.

ambiguity
vague or equivocal language; meaning that can be taken two ways.

antecedent (referent)
the noun for which a pronoun stands.

appositive
a word or phrase that identifies a preceding noun or pronoun: e.g., *Mrs. Jones*, **my aunt**, *is sick*. The second phrase is said to be *in apposition* to the first.

article
a word that precedes a noun and shows whether the noun is definite or indefinite; a kind of determiner or noun-marker.
Indefinite article: *a (an)*.
Definite article: *the*.

assertion
a positive statement or claim: e.g., *The Senate is irrelevant*.

auxiliary
a verb used in combination with another verb to create a verb phrase; a helping verb used to create certain tenses and emphases: e.g., *could, do, may, will, have*.

bibliography
(a) a list of works referred to or found useful in the preparation of an essay or report; **(b)** a reference book listing works available in a particular subject.

case
the inflected form of pronouns (see **inflection**). **Subjective case:** *I, we, he, she, it, they.* **Objective case:** *me, us, him, her, it, them.* **Possessive case:** *my, our, his, her, its, their.*

circumlocution
a roundabout or circuitous expression: e.g., *in a family way* for *pregnant; at this point in time* for *now.*

clause
a group of words containing a subject and predicate. An **independent clause** can stand by itself as a complete sentence: e.g., *I bought a hamburger.* A **subordinate** or **dependent clause** cannot stand by itself but must be connected to another clause: e.g., **Since I was hungry,** *I bought a hamburger.*

cliché
a trite or well-worn expression that has lost its impact through overuse: e.g., *slept like a log, sunny disposition, tried and true.*

collective noun
a noun that is singular in form but refers to a group: e.g., *family, team, jury.* It may take either a singular or a plural verb, depending on whether it refers to individual members or to the group as a whole.

comma splice
see **run-on sentence**.

complement
a completing word or phrase that usually follows a linking verb to form a **subjective complement**: e.g., (1) *He is* **my father**. (2) *That cigar smells* **terrible**. If the complement is an adjective it is sometimes called a **predicate adjective**. An

objective complement completes the direct object rather than the subject: e.g., *We found him* **honest and trustworthy**.

complex sentence
a sentence containing a dependent clause as well as an independent one: e.g., *I bought the ring, although it was expensive.*

compound sentence
a sentence containing two or more independent clauses: e.g., *I saw the car wreck and I reported it.* A sentence is called **compound-complex** if it contains a dependent clause as well as two independent ones: e.g., *When the fog lifted, I saw the car wreck and I reported it.*

conclusion
the part of an essay in which the findings are pulled together or implications revealed so that the reader has a sense of closure or completion.

concrete language
specific language, giving particular details (often details of sense): e.g., *red corduroy dress, three long-stemmed roses* (cf. **abstract language**).

conjunction
an uninflected word used to link words, phrases, or clauses. A **coordinating conjunction** (e.g., *and, or, but, for, yet*) links two equal parts of a sentence. A **subordinating conjunction**, placed at the beginning of a subordinate clause, shows the logical dependence of that clause on another: e.g., (1) **Although** *I am poor, I am happy.* (2) **While** *others slept, he studied.* **Correlative conjunctions** are pairs of coordinating conjunctions (see **correlatives**).

conjunctive adverb
a type of adverb that shows the logical relation between the phrase or clause that it modifies and a preceding one: e.g., (1) *I sent the letter; it never arrived,*

however. (2) *The battery died;* **therefore** *the car wouldn't start.*

connotation
associative meaning; the range of suggestion called up by a certain word. Apparent synonyms, such as *poor* and *underprivileged*, may have different connotations (cf. **denotation**).

context
the text surrounding a particular passage that helps to establish its meaning.

contraction
a word formed by combining and shortening two words: e.g., *isn't, can't, we're.*

coordinate construction
see **correlatives.**

coordinating conjunction
see **conjunction.**

copula verb
see **linking verb.**

correlatives (coordinates)
pairs of coordinating conjunctions: e.g., *either/or, neither/nor, not only/but.*

dangling modifier
a modifying word or phrase (often a participial phrase) that is not grammatically connected to any part of the sentence: e.g., **Walking to school,** *the street was slippery.*

demonstrative pronoun
a pronoun that points out something: e.g., (1) **This** *is his reason.* (2) **That** *looks like my lost earring.* When used to modify a noun or pronoun, a demonstrative pronoun becomes a kind of **pronominal adjective**: e.g., *this hat, those people.*

denotation
the literal or dictionary meaning of word (cf. **connotation**).

diction
the choice of words with regard to their tone, degree of formality, or register. Formal diction is the language of orations

and serious essays. The informal diction of everyday speech or conversational writing can, at its extreme, become slang.

discourse
talk, either oral or written. **Direct discourse** gives the actual words spoken or written: e.g., *Donne said,* **"No man is an island."** In writing, direct discourse is put in quotation marks. **Indirect discourse** gives the meaning of the speech rather than the actual words. In writing, indirect discourse is not put in quotation marks: e.g., *He said that no one exists in an island of isolation.*

ellipsis marks
three spaced periods indicating an omission from a quoted passage.

endnote
a footnote or citation placed at the end of an essay or report.

essay
a literary composition on any subject. Some essays are descriptive or narrative, but in an academic setting most are expository (explanatory) or argumentative.

expletive
a grammatically meaningless exclamation or phrase. The most common expletives are the sentence beginnings *It is* and *There is (are).*

exploratory writing
the informal writing done to help generate ideas before formal planning begins.

footnote
a citation placed at the bottom of a page or the end of the composition (cf. **endnote**).

fused sentence
see **run-on sentence.**

general language
language lacking specific details; abstract language.

gerund
a verbal (part-verb) that functions as a noun and is marked by an *-ing* ending: e.g., **Swimming** *can help you become fit.*

grammar
a study of the forms and relations of words, and of the rules governing their use in speech and writing.

hypothesis
a supposition or trial proposition made as a starting point for further investigation. The plural is *hypotheses*.

hypothetical instance
a supposed occurrence; often shown by a clause beginning with *if*.

indefinite article
a (an). Definite article: *the*.

independent clause
see **clause**.

indirect discourse
see **discourse**.

infinitive
a type of verbal not connected to any subject: e.g., *to ask*. The **base infinitive** omits the *to*: e.g., *ask*.

inflection
the change in the form of a word to indicate number, person, case, tense, or degree.

integrate
combine or blend together.

intensifier (qualifier)
a word that modifies and adds emphasis to another word or phrase: e.g., **very** *tired*, **quite** *happy*, *I* **myself**.

interjection
a remark or exclamation interposed or thrown into a speech, usually accompanied by an exclamation mark: e.g., *Oh dear! Alas!*

interrogative sentence
a sentence that asks a question: e.g., *What is the time?*

intransitive verb
a verb that does not take a direct object: e.g., *fall, sleep, talk*.

italics
slanting type used for emphasis, replaced in typescript by underlining.

jargon
technical terms used unnecessarily or in inappropriate places: e.g., *peer-group interaction* for *friendship*.

linking verb (copula verb)
the verb *to be* used to join subject to complement: e.g., *The apples* **were** *ripe*.

literal meaning
the primary, or denotative, meaning of a word.

logical indicator
a word or phrase — usually a conjunction or conjunctive adverb — that shows the logical relation between sentences or clauses: e.g., *since, furthermore, therefore*.

modifier
a word or group of words that describes or limits another element in the sentence. A **misplaced modifier** causes confusion because it is not placed next to the element it should modify: e.g., *I only ate the pie*. [Revised: *I ate only the pie*.]

mood
(a) as a grammatical term, the form that shows a verb's function (indicative, imperative, interrogative, or subjunctive); **(b)** when applied to literature generally, the state of mind or feeling shown.

non-restrictive element
see **restrictive element**

noun
an inflected part of speech marking a person, place, thing, idea, action, or feeling, and usually serving as subject, object, or complement. A **common** noun

is a general term: e.g., *dog, paper, automobile*. A **proper noun** is a specific name: e.g., *Mary, Sudbury, Skidoo*.

object
(a) a noun or pronoun that, when it completes the action of a verb, is called a **direct object**: e.g., *He passed the* **puck**. An **indirect object** is the person or thing receiving the direct object: e.g., *He passed the* **puck** (direct object) *to* **Richard** (indirect object). **(b)** The noun or pronoun in a group of words beginning with a preposition; pronouns take the objective case: e.g., *at the* house, *about* **her**, *for* **me**.

objective complement
see **complement**.

objectivity
a disinterested stance; a position taken without personal bias or prejudice (cf. **subjectivity**).

outline
with regard to an essay or report, a brief sketch of the main parts; a written plan.

paragraph
a unit of sentences arranged logically to explain or describe an idea, event, or object; usually marked by indentation of the first line.

parallel wording
wording in which a series of items has a similar grammatical form: e.g., *At her marriage my grandmother promised* **to love, to honour, and to obey** *her husband*.

paraphrase
restate in different words.

parentheses
curved lines, enclosing and setting off a passage; not to be confused with square brackets.

parenthetical element
an interrupting word or phrase: e.g., *My musical career,* **if it can be called that,**
consisted of playing the triangle in kindergarten.

participle
a verbal (part-verb) that functions as an adjective. Participles can be either **present**, usually marked by an *-ing* ending (e.g. *taking*), or **past** (*having taken*); they can also be passive (*having been taken*).

parts of speech
the major classes of words. Some grammarians include only function words (nouns, verbs, adjectives, and adverbs); others also include pronouns, prepositions, conjunctions, and interjections.

passive voice
see **voice**.

past participle
see **participle**.

periodic sentence
a sentence in which the normal order is inverted or an essential element suspended until the very end: e.g., *Out of the house, past the grocery store, through the school yard and down the railroad tracks* **raced the frightened boy**.

person
in grammar, the three classes of personal pronouns referring to the person speaking (first person), person spoken to (second person), and person spoken about (third person). With verbs (except for *to be*), only the third person singular has a distinctive form.

personal pronoun
see **pronoun**.

phrase
a unit of words lacking a subject-predicate combination. The most common kind is the **prepositional phrase** — a unit comprising preposition plus object. Some modern grammarians also refer to the **single-word phrase**.

plural
indicating two or more in number. Nouns, pronouns, and verbs all have plural forms.

possessive case
see **case**.

prefix
a syllable placed in front of the root form of a word to make a new word: e.g., *pro-*, *in-*, *sub-* (cf. **suffix**).

preposition
a short word heading a unit of words containing an object, thus forming a **prepositional phrase**: e.g., **under** *the tree*, **before** *my time*.

pronoun
a word that stands in for a noun. A **personal pronoun** stands in for the name of a person: *I, he, she, we, they*, etc.

punctuation
a conventional system of signs used to indicate stops or divisions in a sentence and to make meaning clearer: e.g., comma, period, semicolon, etc.

reference works
material consulted when preparing an essay or report.

referent (antecedent)
the noun for which a pronoun stands.

register
the degree of formality in word choice and sentence structure.

relative clause
a clause headed by a relative pronoun: e.g. *the man* **who came to dinner** *is my uncle.*

relative pronoun
who, which, what, that, or their compounds beginning an adjective or noun clause: e.g., *the house* **that** *Jack built*; **whatever** *you say.*

restrictive element
a phrase or clause that identifies or is essential to the meaning of a term: e.g., *The book* **that I need** *is lost.* It should not be set off by commas. A non-restrictive element is not needed to identify the term and is usually set off by commas: e.g., *The book,* **which I got from my aunt,** *is one of my favourites.*

run-on sentence
a sentence that goes on beyond the point where it should have stopped. The term covers both the **comma splice** (two sentences joined by a comma) and the **fused sentence** (two sentences joined without any punctuation between them).

sentence
a grammatical unit that includes both a subject and a predicate. The end of a sentence is marked by a period.

sentence fragment
a group of words lacking either a subject or a verb; an incomplete sentence.

simple sentence
a sentence made up of only one clause: e.g., *Joan climbed the tree.*

slang
colloquial speech, not considered part of standard English; often used in a special sense by a particular group: e.g., *gross* for *disgusting*; *gig* as a musician's term.

split infinitive
a construction in which a word is placed between *to* and the base verb: e.g., *to completely finish.*

squinting modifier
a kind of misplaced modifier; one that could be connected to elements on either side, making meaning ambiguous: e.g., *When he wrote the letter* **finally** *his boss thanked him.*

standard English
the English currently spoken or written

by literate people over a wide geographical area.

subject
in grammar, the noun or noun equivalent about which something is predicated; that part of a clause with which the verb agrees: e.g., **They** *swim every day when the* **pool** *is open.*

subjective complement
see **complement**.

subjectivity
a personal stance, not impartial (cf. **objectivity**).

subordinate clause
see **clause**.

subordinating conjunction
see **conjunction**.

subordination
making one clause in a sentence dependent on another.

suffix
an addition placed at the end of a word to form a derivative: e.g., *prepare—preparation*; *sing—singing* (cf. **prefix**).

synonym
a word with the same dictionary meaning as another word: e.g., *begin* and *commence.*

syntax
sentence construction; the grammatical relations of words.

tense
the time reference of verbs.

theme
a recurring or dominant idea.

thesis statement
a one-sentence assertion that gives the central argument of an essay or thesis.

topic sentence
the sentence in a paragraph (usually at the start) that expresses the main or controlling idea.

transition word
a word that shows the logical relation between sentences or parts of a sentence and thus helps to signal the change from one idea to another: e.g., *therefore, also, accordingly.*

transitive verb
one that takes an object: e.g., *hit, bring, cover.*

usage
accepted practice.

verb
that part of a predicate expressing an action, state of being, or condition, telling what a subject is or does. Verbs inflect to show tense (time). The principal parts of a verb are the three basic forms from which all tenses are made: the base infinitive, the past tense, and the past participle (e.g., *sing, sang, sung*).

verbal
a word that is similar in form to a verb but does not function as one: a participle, a gerund, or an infinitive.

voice
the form of a verb that shows whether the subject acted (active voice) or was acted upon (passive voice: e.g., *He* **hit** *the ball* (active). *The ball* **was hit** *by him* (passive). Only transitive verbs (verbs taking objects) can be passive.

Index

correlative, 126
subordinating, 96, 126
connotations, 71-2
contractions, 6, 121
correlatives (coordinate constructions),
84, 103, 127
Council of Biology Editors (CBE), 45, 70

dash, 110-11
data, falsification of, 16, 19
databases
CD-ROM, 13
online, 12-13
"table of contents," 14
dates, 109
defining, 34
denotation, 71
descriptors, 13-14
discourse
direct, 111
indirect, 98
documentation, 65-70
see also references

editing, 37-9
ellipsis, 64, 115
emphasis, 82, 116
essay/research paper
conclusion, 37
introduction, 33, 36
length, 5-6
organization, 3, 25, 38-9
outline, 31-3
planning, 24-33
presentation/format, 41, 62
purpose, 4-5
thesis/theme, 29-30, 37
writing, 33-7
see also lab reports
ethical issues
in research, 16, 17-18, 44
in writing, 16, 19-23
evidence, 3-4, 8
see also research
examinations
essay, 89, 90-2
multiple-choice, 89, 92
open-book, 92-3
preparing for, 86-9

take-home, 93
exclamation mark, 111
experiments. See lab reports; research
projects

fabrication, 19
figures, 52, 55-9
APA guidelines, 58-9
see also charts; graphs
focus, 75-6, 80-1
footnotes, 51, 65
fractions, 114
fraud
academic, 19-23
scientific, 16
see also plagiarism
funnel approach, 36, 37

gender, 84, 100
gerund, 101, 128
graphs
bar, 55, 56
line, 56-7
see also charts; figures

headings, 62-3
hyphen, 113-15
hypothesis
experimental, 46, 47, 59, 128
see also thesis
hypothetical instances, 98, 124, 128

index cards, 28-9, 31
indexes
book, 9
citation, 11-12
Index of Scientific Reviews, 10
subject heading, 9
Internet, 14, 15
italics, 62, 111, 115-16

jargon, 6-7, 72, 128
journals, 9, 14
abstract, 10-11
citing articles, 68-9, 70
index, 10-11

keywords, 13-14, 31

lab reports, 5, 6
abstract, 46, 48